IMAGES
of America

CENTRAL FLORIDA'S
WORLD WAR II VETERANS

This illustration of the Iwo Jima Memorial was sketched exclusively for *Central Florida's World War II Veterans* by renowned illustrator and Korean War veteran Norval E. Packwood Jr. Born in Chicago in 1928, Packwood entered the Marine Corps on June 23, 1948. He was a combat artist for the *Marine Corps Gazette* and is the creator of the humorous cartoon character Leatherhead. (Courtesy of artist Gene Packwood.)

ON THE COVER: Bernie Devore, standing on the far left, recalled, "We got into formation and headed to Germany. Our 18th mission had begun. I was scared that our luck had run out and this would be our last. I remembered my mother always praying, but I didn't know how. 'If there is a God, please reveal Yourself to me,' I said. Then a voice spoke to me, 'Relax my son, I will take care of you.' We finished the mission and returned safely." (Courtesy of Bernard Devore.)

IMAGES

of America

CENTRAL FLORIDA'S
WORLD WAR II VETERANS

Bob Grenier

ARCADIA
PUBLISHING

Published by Arcadia Publishing
Charleston, South Carolina

Printed in the United States of America

Library of Congress Control Number: 2015959216

For all general information, please contact Arcadia Publishing:
Telephone 843-853-2070
Fax 843-853-0044
E-mail sales@arcadiapublishing.com
For customer service and orders:
Toll-Free 1-888-313-2665

Visit us on the Internet at www.arcadiapublishing.com

*With gratitude, honor, and love, I dedicate this book to my
dad, a member of the 33rd Division, 121st Tank Battalion,
Illinois National Guard, from 1947 to 1957.*

CONTENTS

ACKNOWLEDGMENTS

I am very grateful to everyone who made this photographic journey through Central Florida's history possible. As you venture through *Central Florida's World War II Veterans*, you will see the names of the many people who have contributed to this work. I am grateful to all these individuals and families, as well as the many fine organizations, for their kind contributions.

Also, there are many honorable mentions, including Maria Trippe, Lois Murphy, Carolyn McGraw, Sheila Tindle, Kay McGee, Myrtice Young, Patrick Lombardi, Leila and Angel Luis Mendoza, Bernie Devore, Frank Clark, Jean Witherington, Olive Horning, Bill Cumbaa, Rebecca Williams, Sandy Mott, Judy Rainey, Edward Quigley, Glenn Christians, Mary Booth, Ray Burtoft, Ric Baysinger, Howard King, Carolyn Sender, Miriam Butler, Don Fuller, Jim McGee, Mary Jo and Mal Martin, Shirley Cannon, Harold Bradeen, Gene Storz, Chuck Downey, Elmer Pegram, Juaneta and Clarence Hershberger, Prof. Wenxian Zhang and Darla Moore of Rollins College, Bob Gasche, Fred Donaldson, Florence McCann, George Hausold, Bob Moody, Betty Lou Forbes, Sam Scott, Carolyn and Claude Mills, Pennie and Leon Olliff, Desta Horner, Lynn Mays, Robert Redd, Margorie Grinnell, Arthur Dreves, Shirley Meade, John Thrasher, Sam Barber, Carey Baker, Jeff Hosterman, Richard Keith, Gene Packwood, Zelia Sweett, David Porter, my sister Dina Peterson, and Rick Brumby of the Museum of Military History.

There are many outstanding organizations to thank, including Polk County History Center, St. Cloud Heritage Museum, Greater Dunnellon Historical Society, Micanopy Historical Society Archives, Geneva Historical Society, Oviedo Historical Society, New Smyrna Museum of History, Zellwood Historical Society, East Lake Historical Society, Leesburg Heritage Society, Lake County Historical Society, Pine Castle Historical Society, Veterans Memorial Center, DeLand Naval Air Station Museum, and the State Archives of Florida.

I thank Liz Gurley at Arcadia Publishing for her patience, support, and faith in me; Alma Grenier for her invaluable research, creative photography, and sound suggestions; and Tavares Public Library reference librarian Marli Wilkins for her extensive, in-depth research, photography, editing, proofreading, and her veteran library skills.

This book was made possible by the support and encouragement of my mom and dad, Wahine, Flash, Capt. Melton Haynes, and of course, God!

INTRODUCTION

I fear all we have done is to awaken a sleeping giant and fill him with a terrible resolve.
—Japanese admiral Isoroku Yamamoto, following the attack on Pearl Harbor

As an author, my main focus was writing about the Florida frontier and the War Between the States. So when I began my quest to write this book, I immediately realized I knew very little about World War II and that period of time—except that I love movies from the 1940s. I knew with each passing day, we are losing more and more of our World War II veterans. So I wanted to pay tribute to them by writing this book, *Central Florida's World War II Veterans*.

I traveled throughout Central Florida to visit with veterans, many of whom are in their nineties, to interview them about their experiences. Each veteran had their own unique story. While in their homes scanning photographs and taking notes, their heartfelt reminiscences began to touch me deeply. I did my very best to stay strong in front of them, but on many occasions, I found myself with tears in my eyes on my drive home.

When I sat down to write about these incredible people, I remembered those interviews, and emotions once again filled my senses, including fear of the possibility that I may never see them again. I had these same deep, patriotic feelings when I visited monuments, memorials, and gravesites.

Unlike the veterans I wrote about in my *Central Florida's Civil War Veterans* book, with this work, I actually had the opportunity to meet and talk with people who stormed beaches, dive-bombed enemy ships, nursed the wounded, fought in the trenches, were prisoners of war, and who raised our flag in liberation. I shall never forget them!

Celebrated international figures, such as Franklin Delano Roosevelt, Dwight David Eisenhower, George Patton, Douglas MacArthur, Chester Nimitz, and Winston Churchill, as well as infamous international figures, such as Adolf Hitler, Benito Mussolini, and Showa Hirohito, were topping the headlines as they commanded armies all over the world, while the names of our sons and daughters, neighbors and friends, such as Bernie Devore, Eugene Olliff, George Hausold, Arthur Dreves, Angel Mendoza, Florence Chromulak, Chuck Downey, Marcus McDilda, and USS *Indianapolis* survivor Clarence Hershberger, gave their last full measure without national fanfare. The following is from Hershberger's unpublished book, *The USS* Indianapolis *CA-35 Tragedy: As Seen by One Survivor*, and is a brief recollection of his five nights at sea:

> Sitting down on my blanket, which is now stretched out on the deck, I proceeded to take off my shoes. Then stretching out on my blanket, I thought to myself, 'now for some well-deserved sleep.' Sleeping topside that night would prove to be a blessing in disguise, for a full night's sleep this Sunday night was not to be.
>
> Shortly after midnight, I and everyone else that had been sleeping were awakened. The explosions threw me several feet in the air. As I opened my eyes, while still in mid-air, the

very first thing that I noticed was this pillar of smoke and flame shooting straight up into the night sky. Upon hitting the deck of the ship about half stunned, and soaking wet, I sat upright. Why I was wet I can only imagine. So I headed aft to my quarters, two decks down, whereupon I changed out of my wet clothes, hanging them over some pipes to dry. I wonder if they are still there.

Picking up my life jacket, I proceeded to work my way topside as the Indy was by now, nearing her death more and more every second. You could actually hear her 'death rattle' now.

Now as I shove off from my perch on the hull of the ship, I proceeded downward, putting my fate in the hands of 'Our heavenly Father.' However as it turned out, I realized later, our 'Lord Jesus' had been with me throughout the ordeal, from beginning to the present. It was almost as if my being soaking wet earlier was, in fact, a sort of 'Baptism.'

Now as I hit the water, I must have 'blacked out' for I felt the sensation of going down into the sea for what seemed like thousands of feet, and a considerable period of time. Then suddenly I realized I was back on the surface covered completely with oil. Rubbing oil from my eyes, I saw chaos everywhere. Men were yelling, screaming, and swimming towards one another. Others were vomiting, crying, and trying hard for some sort of sanity to the almost impossible situation that we now found ourselves to be in. The remainder of the night was spent calling out to one another, trying to gather ourselves into a large group. Toward daybreak our thoughts turned to yet another threat. As was the custom by the Japanese, the sub would surface at first light and machine gun all survivors.

We heard someone yell out, 'Shark!' The sharks were definitely there now, and would remain throughout the whole ordeal, presenting a constant threat to us all. Having their way with whomever they choose, whenever it was to their liking. We were at their mercy, almost all the time. Sometimes warding them off with yelling or splashing worked, when it didn't, well it was simply 'so long Joe' or whatever his name was. One would know from listening to the screams as they attacked one individual, and then yet another, throughout those five terrifying days. The most terrifying part of the whole ordeal was from fellow shipmates going berserk. The chilly fourth night only added to our despair.

Then suddenly around 2200 hours someone shouted out, 'there's a light out there on the horizon! See it!' Then somebody else replied, 'yes, I see it, Jesus is coming!' We could hardly believe it, we were finally being rescued.

Central Florida's World War II Veterans' final chapter, Florida's Gallant Sons and Daughters, is composed of additional images from our featured counties, as well as exciting photographs from every corner of the Florida peninsula. Also included in this exciting bonus chapter are historical tidbits and fun facts about Florida's ties to the war, as well as just a few of the many dedicated people who preserve, educate, and honor the memory of our World War II veterans.

People from all over the world travel to Central Florida to experience the thrilling theme parks and attractions, where they can dance and sing with cartoon characters, save the world with the latest costumed superheroes, ride upside-down on corkscrew roller-coasters, and get splashed by performing dolphins—usually only after waiting hours in a long, interweaving cue line. But Central Florida offers much more! Fascinating history is hidden in plain sight, so keep your eyes open! The area is home to many county and municipal historical societies, museums, state parks, heritage trails, monuments, memorials, and historic sites. The author encourages his readers to visit these places to learn more about the men and women who settled their communities and their roles in Central Florida's history. And take some time to chat with and say thank you to a veteran.

One

POLK COUNTY
BY THEIR SUPERB
COURAGE AND HEROISM

On December 26, 1944, Pvt. James Richard Hendrix, while under heavy fire, distinguished himself on several occasions when he rescued wounded and trapped soldiers and captured German soldiers in Belgium during the Battle of the Bulge. Hendrix served in the US Army, 4th Armored Division and received the Medal of Honor for his actions. He was born in Lepanto, Arkansas, and lived in Davenport, where this monument is located. (Courtesy of the Polk County History Center.)

Cpl. James Henry Mills was the only Polk County native to receive the Medal of Honor. He received the medal for his actions on May 24, 1944, near Cisterna di Littoria, Italy. As an infantry scout, he enabled his platoon to reach the designated spot undiscovered, from which position it assaulted and overwhelmed the enemy, capturing 22 German soldiers and taking the objective without casualties. Mills was born in the Brewster/Fort Meade area. He enlisted in the US Army in 1943 and served in the 3rd Infantry Division. He returned to Fort Meade after being wounded in Italy. Upon returning home, Gov. Spessard Holland and the Polk County citizens welcomed him back with a ceremony outside the courthouse in Bartow. (Left, courtesy of the State Archives of Florida; below, courtesy of the Polk County History Center.)

Spessard Holland was born in Bartow in 1892. During World War II, he served as the 28th governor of Florida. His family was very active in the Florida war effort, including his daughter Mary Groover, who belonged to the Ground Observer Corps. From left to right are Mary Groover, Spessard Jr., wife Mary Agnes, Ivanhoe Elizabeth, Gov. Spessard Holland, Billy Ben, and Mike the family dog. (Courtesy of the Polk County History Center.)

Freddie Tucker Wright and Orrin Hugh Wright served in the US Navy. Freddie was a nurse and Hugh was a torpedo and engineering officer. The Bartow residents met aboard a submarine in Pearl Harbor and were married in San Francisco in 1946. Hugh was a mining engineer and was involved in the phosphate industry. Freddie was a cofounder of the Polk County Historical Association. (Courtesy of the Polk County History Center.)

Pierce native J.J. Corbett was drafted into the Army in January 1943. Corbett served in the 555th Parachute Infantry Battalion, nicknamed the "Triple Nickels." The 555th was one of the few all-black units with black officers. When the Japanese launched fire balloons toward the United States, striking Western states, the 555th became the first "smoke jumpers," jumping out of airplanes to extinguish the fires. (Courtesy of the Polk County History Center.)

Claude Earnest Woodruff Jr. served in the Marines from 1944 to 1946, spending over a year in Japan. After the war, Woodruff graduated from Florida A&M University on a football scholarship. He then returned to his hometown of Bartow and taught and coached at Union Academy. In a long career as a football coach, 12 of his graduates went on to play for the National Football League (NFL). (Courtesy of the Polk County History Center.)

Maynard Chapman Leetun enlisted in the US Army Air Corps in Webster Groves, Missouri. Leetun was assigned to the B-24 Heavy Bomber Squadron's 98th Bombardment Group, where he was promoted to staff sergeant. He completed 52 missions in his Liberator bomber, which was nicknamed "Misbehavin." Leetun participated in the Po Valley, Schweinfurt, and Ploesti raids and received an Air Medal for meritorious achievement in aerial combat. (Courtesy of the Polk County History Center.)

The Brown brothers are, from left to right, (sitting) Council, also known as "Coot;" (standing) Clyde, A. Glenn, and Pete. Prompted by the attack on Pearl Harbor, A. Glenn Brown enlisted in the Navy on January 6, 1942. He was a gunner's mate on the Danish merchant ship *Nordvest*, which he had shipped out on immediately following basic training. A. Glenn eventually qualified as an aviator. In November 1945, he was promoted to ensign. (Courtesy of A. Glenn Brown.)

Harold "Hal" Sanborn served in the Army Air Corps as an intelligence photographer under Gen. Douglas MacArthur in the Philippines. Sanborn was one of the first to fly over and photograph the cities of Hiroshima and Nagasaki after the atomic bombs exploded in August 1945, capturing the aftermath from an open cockpit. Sanborn's brother Dan, who was also a photographer, served in the Navy as an intelligence photographer. (Courtesy of Carlton Phelps.)

Forrest Elwood "Rocky" Sawyer served in the Navy and is a survivor of the USS *Yorktown* in the Battle of Midway. He is the recipient of many awards, including the Presidential Unit Citation. His bride, Lakeland native Floy Mize Sawyer, served in the US Marine Corps Women's Reserve. Pictured at their 1945 wedding are, from left to right, Patsy Harp Lombardi, Rocky, Floy, unidentified, and Pastor C.N. Walker. (Courtesy of Phyllis Mallory Kendrick Hammond.)

John Lemuel "J.L." Costine, pictured with his wife, Louise Walker Costine, was a tank technical sergeant in the 10th Armored Division, nicknamed the "Tiger Division," under the command of Gen. George Patton and, later, Gen. Alexander "Sandy" Patch. Costine served in France and Germany. He seized a pistol from a German colonel, which remains in the possession of the Costine family today. (Courtesy of Lois Sherrouse Murphy.)

Brothers James R. "J.R." and Elmon Sherrouse (Elmon spelled family name with only one 'r') enlisted in the Army in January 1942. Elmon deployed overseas, serving in France in the Glider infantry, but J.R. was turned back three times because of a heart condition. J.R. was a technician fifth grade with the 3651st Ordnance Heavy Automotive Maintenance Company for over two years when he was discharged on December 9, 1944. (Courtesy of Lois Sherrouse Murphy.)

15

After a stint in the Civilian Conservation Corps, William Silas Phelps entered the Army. He spent most of his tour in Italy, where he transported supplies and ammunition to men fighting in the mountains. When night fell, they used mules to transport the provisions up the slopes. On one occasion, while on patrol, a German soldier emerged from a hedge row to surrender himself to Phelps. (Courtesy of Carlton Phelps.)

Robert Lusk, pictured with his wife, Laura, in 2015, joined the Navy in 1942. After completing gunnery school, Lusk was assigned to an LCT (landing craft tank), transporting troops and supplies to Africa and Italy. While training for the D-Day Normandy invasion, Lusk's name was drawn for leave that sent him home for a month. While home, his LCT crew hit a mine on the beach, which killed most on board. (Courtesy of the Polk County History Center.)

Wilburn Dayton Harp joined the Navy and was deployed into service in 1941. He served aboard the USS *Yorktown* during the Battle of the Coral Sea in May 1942. Harp was awarded the Navy Distinguished Flying Cross from Adm. Chester Nimitz for "heroism and extraordinary achievement while rear gunner of a bombing squadron in action against Japanese forces in the Coral Sea." Harp made bombing attacks on ships at Tulagi Harbor. (Courtesy of Patrick Lombardi.)

David Groves (right) entered the US Army on July 4, 1943, at Camp Blanding. He served in the 19th Armored Infantry Battalion, 14th Armored Division, nicknamed the "Liberators." The division landed at Marseilles, France, in October 1944. The unit liberated over 110,000 allied prisoners from Oflag XIII and Stalag XIII near Hammelburg, Stalag VII near Moosburg, and sub-camps of Dachau. He earned a Purple Heart and two Bronze Stars. (Courtesy of the Polk County History Center.)

Singer and actress Frances Langford grew up in Mulberry, near Lakeland. In 1941, she was asked by Bob Hope to join him on USO tours of Europe, North Africa, and the South Pacific. Langford wrote the weekly newspaper column "Purple Heart Diary," in which she described her visits to hospitals to entertain soldiers and to ask for support that the wounded receive all the necessary supplies. (Courtesy of the State Archives of Florida.)

Gen. James Van Fleet, pictured with Gen. George Patton (left), served in the Mexican border campaign and World War I. At the onset of World War II, he commanded the 8th Infantry Regiment, Fourth Division, XXIII Corps, which was chosen to spearhead the D-Day landing at Utah Beach. By 1944, Van Fleet held a field rank of major general and received the Distinguished Service Cross for extraordinary heroism. (Courtesy of the Polk County History Center.)

Two

OSCEOLA COUNTY
IN DEFENSE OF DEMOCRACY

The Bataan-Corregidor "A Tribute to Courage" Memorial is located in Kissimmee Lakefront Park. The monument inscription reads, "Dedicated to the Americans and Filipinos who served in Defense of Democracy in the Philippines during World War II – especially in Bataan and Corregidor, and on the infamous Death March." The monolith is inscribed with the following quote, given by an unidentified soldier of the Battle of Bataan: "Honor those who died that you might stand here free this day." (Courtesy of Alma Nevarez Grenier.)

The 65th Infantry Veterans Park was dedicated in 2011 by the Osceola County Commission. Located in Buenaventura Lakes, the park honors the 65th Infantry Regiment, a Puerto Rican regiment of the US Army, known as the "Borinqueneers." During World War II, the 65th saw service in Panama, Casablanca, France, and Germany. In November 1943, Col. Antulio Segarra became the first Puerto Rican officer to command a regular Army regiment. (Courtesy of Alma Nevarez Grenier.)

Angel Luis Mendoza, shown in 1950 with his bride, Leila Estrella, entered the Army in 1940. He served with the 65th Infantry Regiment as a machine gunner. In 1943, Mendoza, from Cayey, Puerto Rico, was sent to Panama, where his regiment trained in the extreme heat of the jungle. In 1944, they trained in Virginia before embarking for North Africa. He was in Germany on V-E Day and remembered the exuberant weeklong celebrations. (Courtesy of Leila and Angel Mendoza.)

Carl Tange (left), pictured with L.D. Grifes, was born in Los Angeles in 1926 and enlisted in the Navy in 1944. After boot camp, he trained for 26 weeks in Norman, Oklahoma, as an aviation ordnance man. He was assigned to Carrier Aircraft Service Unit No. 33 in California until June 1945. Tange then served aboard the USS *Hancock* CV-19 aircraft carrier in the Pacific theater of operations. (Courtesy of Carl Tange.)

Charles Mobley was born in Chinquapin, North Carolina, in 1926. He enlisted in the Navy in Wilmington in 1946. Mobley served aboard the auxiliary destroyer USS *Shenandoah* AD-26, which supplied maintenance support for warships. He served on the USS *Shenandoah* during its first tour of duty with the 6th Fleet from June through August 1947. The tour sailed to Gibraltar, Naples, Sardinia, and throughout the Mediterranean area. (Courtesy of Charles Mobley.)

Herman Heil, with his arm around his wife, Adeline McKeon, served in the Army from January 1942 until November 1944. A staff sergeant with Company F, 143rd Infantry, 36th Division, Heil participated in the first wave at Salerno, Italy, and was in the Battle of San Peitro. In 1944, he was awarded the Bronze Star from President Roosevelt and, in 1989, the Conspicuous Service Medal from New York governor Mario Cuomo. (Courtesy of Herman Heil.)

Philip Cook, second from left, is pictured in Germany with fellow soldiers of the 102nd Infantry Division. The 102nd, called the Ozarks, landed at Cherbourg, France, in September 1944 to begin an invasion into Germany. In early 1945, Cook saw action at the Roer River, fought across France to the Rhine River, and then by April, after fighting heavy resistance, reached the Elbe River, less than 50 miles from Berlin. (Courtesy of Philip Cook.)

In 1976, Frank Clark (center) received a meritorious commendation from Capt. E.W. Hille, commanding officer of the Naval Administrative Command in Orlando. Accepting the commendation with Clark are his wife, Ann Wilborn, and daughter Tammy. Lt. Ted White is standing at right. Born in Ruby, South Carolina, Clark served during the European occupation. He was a cofounder of the Veterans Tribute and Museum, chartered June 30, 2004. (Courtesy of Frank Clark.)

On March 31, 2012, the Museum of Military History, located on Irlo Bronson Highway in Kissimmee, opened its doors to the public following a ceremony that dedicated the museum to veterans, those heroes lost in battle, and to Osceola County. The Museum of Military History and its parent company, Veterans Tribute and Museum, were cofounded by Jim and Jerry Kervin and Frank Clark. (Courtesy of the Museum of Military History.)

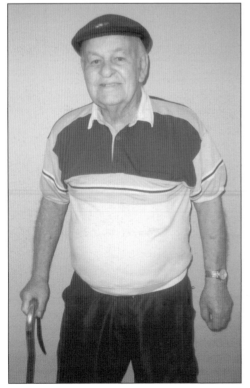

Nick Maropis entered the Army in February 1943. Following an assignment at a trade school, he was sent to the 49th Station Complement Squadron in South Carolina. In August 1943, Maropis deployed to England to the 67th Fighter Wing, 8th Fighter Command Base, to maintain utility systems. He met and married his wife, Mavis Edna Holland, in England. Maropis invented the ultrasonic wrench used by NASA for the Apollo moon expedition in 1969. (Author's collection.)

Roger Thacher sailed to England aboard the HMS *Queen Mary*. On June 6, 1944, Thacher boarded a LST (landing ship tank) and landed at Utah Beach. On the march toward Sainte Mere-Eglise, he took over driving a tank. Along the way, Thacher ran out of gas, drove into a machine gun nest, took a dispatch off of one German soldier and a German Iron Cross from another, and tied a German motorcycle onto the tank. (Author's collection.)

Bernard "Bernie" Devore, a B-17 flight engineer, met his wife, Virginia Saye, in St. Petersburg. The couple had been dating for three months when Devore decided that he did not want her to get away while he was overseas, so they married on May 7, 1944. He shipped out the next morning. Devore, standing on the far left, is seen below with his flight and ground crew; they flew 30 missions. On the 17th mission, his Flying Fortress took a direct hit. The navigator informed the crew that they would crash-land in Germany. Devore did not want to crash in Germany and decided that they needed to drop the ball turret since it created a lot of drag. Two crew members helped Devore drop the turret by giving him oxygen while he removed the bolts. When the turret broke loose, he almost fell through the hole, but the crewmen were able to hold him in. They returned safely to their base. (Both, courtesy of Bernard Devore.)

Pictured are, from left to right, James Buckner, unidentified, and Walter Samolio in 1944. Before Pearl Harbor was bombed, Buckner had shipped out from San Diego aboard the USS *Henderson* with the 4th Defense Battalion of the US Marines. He had been at Pearl Harbor a week when it was bombed. After the attack, Buckner spent two days guarding the oil storage farm. When his ship was ready, they transported cargo to Midway. (Courtesy of the St. Cloud Heritage Museum.)

John Nicholson of St. Cloud first flew over the Normandy coast of France on June 6, 1944, as a tail gunner on a B-26 Marauder bomber. Nicholson remembers the targets on that first mission turned out to be dummies; they were telephone poles set up to look like artillery guns. Later that day, they were sent to bomb a marshalling yard. During the war, Nicholson survived five crash landings. (Courtesy of the St. Cloud Heritage Museum.)

Col. Louis A. Guessaz Jr., pictured here at his retirement on November 30, 1960, was the son of Louis A. Guessaz, publisher of the *St. Cloud News*. At the outbreak of World War II, he was promoted to captain and stationed at Fort Blanding for three years, where he earned a promotion to major. During the war, he served in New Zealand, China, the Philippines, and Japan. (Courtesy of the St. Cloud Heritage Museum.)

Robert Fisk, first row fourth from left, enlisted in the Navy in 1942 and was assigned to the Naval Hospital in Jacksonville. In 1943, he served at the Naval Training Center at Pensacola and the Naval Hospital Corps School in Portsmouth, Virginia. Fisk was stationed at the Carrier Aircraft Service, Unit No. 1, at the naval station in Pearl Harbor from April until December 1945. (Courtesy of the St. Cloud Heritage Museum.)

The Kissimmee Municipal Airport opened in 1940. The following year, the Army took over the airport, and it became known as the Kissimmee Army Airfield. It was used as a training center for fighter and bomber groups. In 1942, the airfield was used for night fighter pilot training. The airfield was closed in July 1945. Pictured is the former Flying Tigers Warbird Restoration Museum. (Courtesy of the State Archives of Florida.)

On the grounds of Makinson-Carson American Legion Post No. 10 in Kissimmee stands a monument to honor the memory of their fallen soldiers. The post was named for local World War I veterans William Thomas Makinson and Nathan Bryan Carson. This photograph features the names of those who served in World Wars I and II. The plaque at the base of the monument reads, "In memory of those who shall have borne the battle." (Courtesy of Alma Nevarez Grenier.)

Three

SUMTER AND LAKE COUNTIES
SPIRIT OF SELF-SACRIFICE

The Florida National Cemetery is located in the Withlacoochee State Forest near Bushnell in Sumter County. It became the fourth national cemetery in Florida and began interments in 1988. Among the notable interments are World War II Navy captain Mike Holovak, who skippered a PT (patrol torpedo) boat credited with sinking nine Japanese ships in the South Pacific, and Col. Leonard Schroeder Jr., the first soldier ashore in the Normandy landings on D-Day. (Author's collection.)

Marine buddies (from left to right) Robert McTureous, Don Mahoney, and Harry McKnight met during infantry training at Camp Lejeune. All three were sent to Okinawa. When they arrived in May 1945, they were separated. On June 5, Mahoney was hit in the chest three times by Japanese fire but survived. On June 7, McTureous's unit suffered casualties taking a hill. As the stretcher-bearers went out to retrieve the wounded, they came under fire. Acting on his own, McTureous filled his shirt with hand grenades and charged the Japanese-occupied caves. He succeeded in drawing the enemy's fire away from the stretcher-bearers but was shot in the stomach. He died four days later on a hospital ship. McTureous received the Medal of Honor for his courageous actions. At left is McTureous with his niece Carolyn in November 1944. (Both, courtesy of Carolyn McTureous Semler.)

On October 24, 1944, while on a route mapping mission with the 20th Combat Mapping Squadron, David Ecoff and his crew spotted Japanese ships near the Philippines. With heavy cloud cover, Ecoff descended to 4,000 feet to take accurate photographs. His airplane was spotted, and immediately, he came under antiaircraft fire. His photographs revealed 50 ships headed to the Leyte Gulf to attack American ships. Ecoff received the Distinguished Flying Cross. (Courtesy of Chuck Varney.)

Edward Hogan, the author's uncle (left), and Don Serwatt served with the 3rd Marine Division. They saw heavy action in the jungles of Guam, as well as Iwo Jima, where the "Fighting Third" delivered the final attack of the operation, a drive to Kitano Point. The division was preparing to invade Japan when the Japanese surrendered. In 1945, they arrived in Japan as part of the occupational forces. (Courtesy of Michael Hogan.)

Robert Baysinger was assigned to the 668th Engineer Topographic Company in 1942. His unit traveled to England in September 1943. Bob and five other men from the Photomapping Platoon were detached to work on a highly classified project. They were referred to as the "Secret Six." Their mission was to create scale terrain models of the D-Day invasion beaches. These models were vital in planning the assault. (Courtesy of Ric Baysinger.)

Arthur King entered the Army in 1942 and served in the Corps of Engineers. In 1944, he was sent to Los Alamos, New Mexico, amidst the shroud of secrecy surrounding the Manhattan Project, the code name for the development of the atom bomb. He worked as an engineering aide under Dr. Robert Oppenheimer, who designed the bomb. King was promoted to tech sergeant prior to the attack on Hiroshima. (Courtesy of Howard King.)

Capt. James McKnight of Fruitland Park enlisted in the Army and was stationed at MacDill Field in Tampa in 1941. He was transferred to England after finishing flight training in early spring 1944, just prior to his daughter Betty Lou's birth in May. He served in the 570th Bomber Squadron participating in air offensives over Europe. McKnight died on a flight mission in 1944, never getting to meet his daughter. (Courtesy of Betty Lou McKnight Forbes.)

Paul Arthur Mott enlisted in the Army Air Corps after graduating from high school in May 1942. Mott's basic training was at Camp Chaffee, Arkansas. He was assigned to a glider unit and did glider pilot training at Fort Sumner, New Mexico. After the glider program was disbanded, Mott was assigned to an Air-Sea Rescue Unit and served with this unit overseas, stationed at Rosneath, Scotland. (Courtesy of Sanda Crabtree Mott.)

MaryLouise Walker Booth
Navy - 1945

Mary Louise "Dixie" Walker Booth and Thomas Edward Booth Jr. met in Groveland after they both were discharged from the Navy and married on December 15, 1946. Mary was visiting a friend in St. Petersburg, and on a whim, went to Tampa to enlist. After boot camp in the Bronx, she was sent to Glenview Naval Air Station for classes in nursing. Mary, a hospital apprentice second class, worked helping servicemen recover in the hospital at Parris Island. Thomas, who was born in Clermont, served in the Pacific theater as a gunner on a destroyer. (Both, courtesy of Mary Louise Booth.)

Thomas Edward Booth Jr.
Navy - 1944

Raymond Burtoft, pictured in Germany in 1945, served in the 8th Tank Battalion, 4th Armored Division, 3rd Army. Burtoft landed in LeHavre and participated in the Battle of the Bulge. He fought through France and into Germany and Czechoslovakia. At Chaumont, France, his battalion sustained a powerful tank-led counterattack. In 2015, Burtoft received France's highest distinction, the Legion of Honor, with the rank of chevalier. (Courtesy of Raymond Burtoft.)

Glenn Christians (second from left) entered the service in 1942 and served as a signalman in the Navy Armed Guard. In 1943, Christians was aboard a ship that provided supplies to the French Resistance. On a volunteer mission with two French sailors, his ship was hit by a mine off the French coast. In 2015, Christians received France's highest distinction, the Legion of Honor, with the rank of chevalier. (Courtesy of Glenn Christians.)

Bill and Carolyn Martin Cumbaa were married on February 3, 1946. Carolyn made her wedding dress out of parachute silk. Cumbaa served in the Marines from 1941 to 1957. In 1943, he went to Pavuvu, the Marine home base in the Pacific. Cumbaa led a platoon against the Japanese at the battles of Peleliu and Okinawa. He received Silver Stars for each battle, two Presidential Unit Citations, and three Purple Hearts. (Courtesy of Carolyn and Bill Cumbaa.)

Edward and Jane Carey Quigley were married on July 14, 1945. On April 6, 1944, Quigley flew his last mission with his B-24 bomber crewmates. They were headed for an airfield outside Brunswick, Germany, when they were hit by a FW 190T fighter. Two engines were destroyed; the plane caught fire and went into a spin. Quigley parachuted into a farm field and became a prisoner of war. (Courtesy of Jane and Edward Quigley.)

Elizabeth Josephine "Betty Jo" Bumgarner, pictured with husband, Jack Garner, served in the Navy as a hospital corpsman during World War II. She received an honorable discharge as a hospital apprentice first class. Betty Jo was the granddaughter of James Lee Hux, Leesburg chief of police, who was killed in the line of duty in 1924. Jack Garner was an actor, golf professional, and the brother of actor James Garner. (Courtesy of Judy Hux Rainey.)

Leighton Baker, pictured with his wife, Ann Elizabeth Brown, was a gun shop owner, statesman, soldier, author, big-game hunter, rancher, and adventurer. He served in the Army with the 79th Infantry Division as an infantry platoon leader. He was wounded near Luneville, France. Baker was elected as state representative to the Florida legislature in 1962, becoming the first Republican to be elected to any office in Lake County. (Courtesy of Carey Baker.)

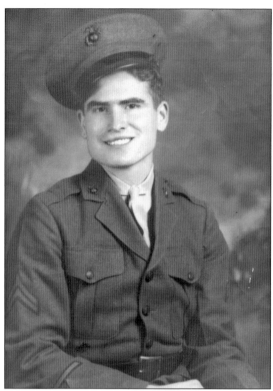

Edward DeRay Phifer entered the Marines on August 19, 1938, after serving two years in the Army in the Panama Canal Zone. Phifer saw action in the Bougainville and Guadalcanal Campaigns, the assault, seizure, and occupation of Guam. In February 1945, he fought up the peak of Mount Suribachi in the Battle of Iwo Jima, Volcano Islands. Phifer married Mazie Margaret Phillips on March 16, 1942. (Courtesy of Rebecca Phifer Williams.)

John Vance "J.V." Phillips enlisted in the Army in January 1941 at Fort McPherson, Georgia. He served with Company K, 121st Infantry, and saw action in Normandy, Northern France, Rhineland, and Central Europe. Phillips was wounded in action twice. This 1990 photograph of Phillips and his sisters and wife was taken at Lake Miona in Oxford. From left to right, the women are Bessie Hood, Geneva Jones, and Mazie Phifer. (Courtesy of Rebecca Phifer Williams.)

Daniel Keel served in the Army Air Corps from 1943 to 1946. He was a navigator, bombardier, triple-rated pilot, and one of the original Tuskegee Airmen. Keel flew several types of aircraft, including the North American P-51 Mustang, the fighter aircraft with which the Tuskegee Airmen were most associated. When the airmen painted the tails of their Thunderbolts and Mustangs red, the distinguished aviators received the nickname "Red Tails." (Artwork by and courtesy of Bob Grenier Sr.)

Marine sergeant J. Hiram Woods received a Bronze Star from Lt. Gen. Holland Smith for leading his section of three amphibious tractors across an open airstrip under heavy Japanese artillery fire to their objective in the foothills of Mount Tapochau in Saipan in 1944. Woods again came under fire for three days as he crossed the channel to Tinian transporting water, rations, and ammunition to the front lines. (Courtesy of Ardelphia Jane Meade Woods.)

Leesburg held regular war bond rallies soon after the Japanese attack on Pearl Harbor on December 7, 1941, until the end of the war. The war bond drive seen here was held in front of the First National bank on Main Street. Leesburg's bond drives featured armament displays and entertainers. More than 85 million Americans purchased over $150 billion in US Treasury war bonds. (Courtesy of the Leesburg Heritage Museum.)

This World War II bond drive was held at Pine Eden, which was the home of Minnie and William Dwight of Fruitland Park. Minnie Dwight hosted this garden party to promote the sale of war bonds. Leesburg legend George Rast is kneeling in front of "Hitler's Casket" and chamber of commerce secretary Wilma Marsh is standing next to him. (Courtesy of the Leesburg Heritage Society.)

Wilson Sheppard, pictured second from right, served as a Navy lieutenant. In this c. 1944 photograph, he is aboard the USS *Isherwood* DD-520 with fellow gunnery officers. Sheppard sailed aboard the destroyer as it cruised the Pacific Ocean making submarine sweeps in the Alaskan waters, taking part in the bombardments of the Kurile Islands, and invading the Philippines and Okinawa. (Courtesy of the Lake County Historical Society.)

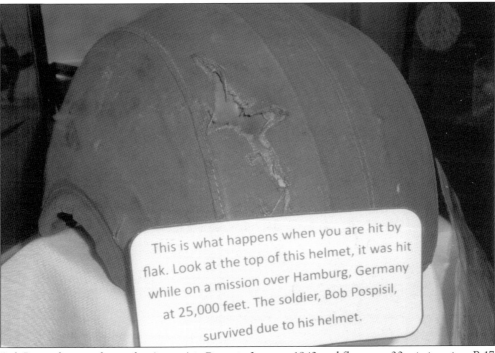

This is what happens when you are hit by flak. Look at the top of this helmet, it was hit while on a mission over Hamburg, Germany at 25,000 feet. The soldier, Bob Pospisil, survived due to his helmet.

Bob Pospisil entered into the Army Air Corps in January 1943 and flew over 30 missions in a B-17 as a waist gunner. A weak right eye prevented him from being a pilot, so he tested as a gunner. Continually failing the tests, he eventually memorized the eye chart. On a mission over Germany, Pospisil was hit by flak from antiaircraft guns. Pictured is the helmet Pospisil wore that saved his life. (Author's collection.)

Virgil Butler (seated far right), with other pilots in his squadron, relaxes in China in 1944. Butler flew with the Flying Tigers in the China-Burma-India theater with the 74th Fighter Squadron. On August 13, 1944, while strafing the shipping in the Xiang River near Hengyang, Butler's engine quit and he landed in a rice paddy. With the aid of the Chinese, he ventured over 100 miles on foot back to his home base at Kweilin. (Courtesy of Miriam Butler.)

Kenneth Ray Williams entered the Army in December 1942 and served in Company F, 338th Infantry Regiment. He received a Silver Star for gallantry in action on May 13, 1944, in Italy. Advancing under heavy artillery and mortar fire and under direct observation by the enemy, Williams and his platoon officer succeeded in driving the enemy from a house from which they were holding up the advance. (Author's collection.)

Lloyd "Clyde" White enlisted in the Navy in May 1943. He was assigned to the Navy Armed Guard aboard merchant ships protecting them from submarines and aircraft. White served in the European, Pacific, and China-Burma-India theaters. He crossed the Atlantic Ocean 12 times and the Indian and Pacific Oceans twice. White participated in the invasion of Anzio on February 1, 1944, and in May 1944 near Malta, his convoy was attacked by German torpedoes. (Courtesy of the Lake County Historical Society.)

On December 7, 1943, two years to the day of the Pearl Harbor attack, Hubert Preston Skipper eloped with Louise Marie Gash. Louise referred to their elopement as a "wartime marriage with a lifetime love affair." Inducted in the Army in Tavares in early 1942, Skipper served in the European theater and participated in the Battle of the Bulge with the 440th Armored Field Artillery Battalion. (Author's collection.)

On the shore of Lake Louisa in Clermont stands this monument to Lt. Dean Gilmore. On November 14, 1944, Gilmore, already a highly decorated pilot and veteran of 91 missions, was on a low-altitude training mission over Lake Louisa when his P51 Mustang suddenly dropped nose first into the water, exploded, and sank. He did not survive. Gilmore received the Distinguished Flying Cross for his actions in Italy in 1944. (Author's collection.)

The 2,800-square-foot Veterans Memorial at Fountain Lake honors veterans from Lake, Sumter, and Marion Counties. It is one of the largest memorials in the Southeast. On May 19, 2012, executive director Donald Van Beck hosted a dedication ceremony. The event included an appearance by the Rolling Thunder, a national veterans' motorcycle group. Speakers included Sen. Carey Baker, Brig. Gen. Tim Sullivan, and Maj. Gen. Polly Peyer. (Author's collection.)

Four

SEMINOLE COUNTY
THE NEED FOR FREEDOM

The Winter Springs Veterans Memorial is located at the corner of Tuskawilla Road and Blumberg Boulevard. The memorial project began in 2005 by the Rotary Club, which wanted to commemorate the local soldiers who have served, or who are currently serving, in the fight for freedom in all theaters of the world. The Rotary Club partnered with the City of Winter Springs to build this extraordinary monument. (Author's collection.)

Leon and Pennie Mitchem Olliff were married in June 1945. Olliff entered the Navy in 1943 and served aboard the USS *William T. Powell* DE-213 destroyer escort. He crossed the hazardous Atlantic many times. On its escort missions, the ship sank mines, defended against submarines, and faced air attacks. Sometime after the war, Olliff became the mayor of Oviedo, and he also operated the city's only barbershop. (Courtesy of Pennie and Leon Olliff.)

Charles Olliff is pictured with his son Randy in 1952. Olliff enlisted in October 1942 and served in the Platoon Leaders Unit and then went to the Naval Training Corps at Duke University. By the end of the war, he was a platoon sergeant at Marine Corps Base Quantico in Virginia. Olliff was a career military man, spending several years in the 1950s in Germany. He achieved the rank of lieutenant colonel. (Courtesy of Pennie and Leon Olliff.)

YOU ARE LEAVING
THE AMERICAN SECTOR
ВЫ ВЫЕЗЖАЕТЕ ИЗ
АМЕРИКАНСКОГО СЕКТОРА
VOUS SORTEZ
DU SECTEUR AMÉRICAIN
SIE VERLASSEN DEN AMERIKANISCHEN SEKTOR
US ARMY

Alfonso Hinojosa, pictured third from left, was a master parachutist of the 503rd Parachute Infantry combat team. He jumped in the parachute attack to recapture Corregidor, Philippines, in February 1945, as well as against the Japanese garrison at Lae, New Guinea, on September 5, 1943. Hinojosa was a sergeant major and a recipient of the Purple Heart. He held security clearance for the Nuremberg Trials. (Courtesy of the Geneva Historical Society.)

Earl P. Summersill, pictured here at Fort Jackson, South Carolina, in 1941, was one of four brothers who served in World War II. Summersill served with the 8th Army Air Corps. His brother Charlie was in the Army and helped build railroads in Europe following D-Day. Brother Myrle was in the Navy and was on a ship that searched for submarines. Brother Thomas served in the Merchant Marines. (Courtesy of the Geneva Historical Society.)

Eddie "Buddy" Banks (left) served in the Army for four years and met and married his wife, Viola, in 1941 while in the service. During training, he was transferred several times while waiting to be shipped overseas but remained in the states. Banks and Viola did not wish to have children while he was in the service—and they did not—but as Banks remarked, "I made up for it. We had ten children." Evans Bacon (below) entered the Army and received his basic training at Fort Lee, Virginia. He then was transferred back to Orlando. Bacon was assigned to the motor pool and was in charge of a group of men in the transportation division. (Both, courtesy of the Geneva Historical Society.)

Sue Miller Smith enlisted in the Army Nurse Corps in 1943. She received basic training at Fort Meade. Smith was assigned to the 93rd General Hospital and moved to Fort Dix to await transportation to England. She crossed on a Cunard-White Star liner, which was stripped of its luxuries. Smith landed in Scotland and then took a train to North Wales. After a month, she moved into a hospital in central England. (Courtesy of the Geneva Historical Society.)

David Harrison Greer was born in Geneva to Isabel and Ben Greer, who had settled near Twin Lakes in 1912. Greer enlisted in the Marine Corps soon after the attack on Pearl Harbor. He served in the Pacific theater, including New Caledonia, Guam, and Guadalcanal. Following the war, he and his wife, Virginia, settled in Fort Walton, Florida, where he worked at Eglin Air Force Base as the chief maintenance officer. (Courtesy of the Geneva Historical Society.)

Edward Baxter enlisted in the Marine Corps and trained at Parris Island. Baxter had recalled that during his stay at boot camp, the Japanese were considered the main enemy. After graduating sea school in Virginia, he was placed on the naval transport ship USS *Henderson* and traveled throughout Asia. This 2002 photograph shows Baxter standing next to the statue of his grandfather Francis Baxter at the Orange County Regional History Center. (Courtesy of the Geneva Historical Society.)

James Galloway, seated in the first row, third from right, enlisted in the Army at Camp Blanding on April 9, 1943, where he received his active-duty training. Born in Seminole County in 1923, Galloway served for the duration of the war. Black soldiers and airmen served with such high distinction during World War II that Pres. Harry Truman issued an executive order in July 1948 desegregating all US armed forces. (Courtesy of the Geneva Historical Society.)

William Mark Earnest, pictured at right with his bride, Patricia Baker Earnest, and below center with two Air Force buddies, served as a fighter pilot in the Army Air Corps. He flew with the 85th Fighter Squadron of the 79th Fighter Group. Lieutenant Earnest received the Distinguished Flying Cross for extraordinary achievement leading a squadron of 11 P-40s over Bojano, Italy, in 1943. After he released his bombs with devastating effect, he dove to a low level through intense ground fire and destroyed six gun positions, which enabled the other pilots to complete their mission and inflict heavy casualties. After the war, Earnest trained pilots for the Korean War in the F-86 Saber. (Both, courtesy of Walter Earnest.)

R. GRENIER

Hedy Lamarr was a legendary movie actress of the 1930s and 1940s. She was also among the most notable women inventors of the 20th century and a pioneer in wireless communications. At the onset of World War II, Lamarr and composer George Anthiel developed "spread spectrum" and frequency hopping technology to prevent the enemy from jamming guided torpedoes and prevent classified messages from being intercepted. They received their patent in 1941. The technology was not utilized until the Cuban Missile Crisis in 1962, and it eventually emerged in various military applications. Their spread spectrum technology was the foundation for today's cellular telephones, fax machines, Wi-Fi, and Bluetooth technology. Lamarr also helped raise millions of dollars for war bonds and washed dishes at USOs. She starred in many films during the war years, including *H.M. Pulham, Esq.* in 1941, costarring Robert Young; *Tortilla Flat* in 1942, with Spencer Tracy; and the 1944 American World War II spy film, *The Conspirators*, with Paul Henreid. Lamarr lived in Altamonte Springs and Casselberry from 1990 until her passing in 2000. (Artwork by and courtesy of Bob Grenier Sr.)

Five

ORANGE COUNTY
THE GREATEST BATTLE EVER FOUGHT

The Central Florida Veterans Memorial Park at Lake Nona was dedicated on November 11, 2013, and honors those who left Central Florida and never returned, as well as helps heal those who did come home. This memorial honors over 1,000 veterans from Orange, Lake, Brevard, Osceola, Seminole, and Volusia Counties who made the ultimate sacrifice in World War I, World War II, Korea, Vietnam, the Persian Gulf, Somalia, Afghanistan, Iraq, and Operation New Dawn. (Author's collection.)

From left to right, George Brown, Arthur Dreves, and Walter Nykiell stand in front of a tomb on Okinawa in September 1945. Dreves enlisted in November 1941. In 1944, after a short stint with the Edison Raiders of the 1st Marine Raiders Battalion, he joined the 1st Marine Division at Pavuvu. He participated in the amphibious assault of Peleliu on September 15, 1944, and landed at Okinawa on Easter Sunday, April 1, 1945. (Courtesy of Arthur Dreves.)

Navy veteran Shirley Rudler is pictured around 1943 in Orlando. In July 1942, Pres. Franklin Roosevelt signed a law that created the women's branch of the Navy, the Women Accepted for Voluntary Emergency Service (WAVES). Soon after, the Women's Auxiliary Army Corps (WAAC) was refashioned as the Women's Army Corps (WAC) and the Women's Auxiliary Ferrying Squadron (WAFS), and Semper Paratus Always Ready Service (SPARS), the US Coast Guard Women's Reserve, were formed. (Courtesy of the State Archives of Florida.)

Charles Grinnell entered the Army in 1941. After serving in various engineering battalions, as well as graduating from officer candidate school in 1942, Grinnell was assigned to Fort Pierce Naval Amphibious Training Base from November 1943 to February 1944. He embarked for Europe on March 3, 1944, and landed at Bristol, England. While serving in the engineering corps in General Patton's 3rd Army, Grinnell built bridges for troop movement across Europe. (Courtesy of Marjorie Grinnell.)

Tom Staley entered the Navy directly after graduating high school in 1943. After basic training at Great Lakes and 12 weeks training in Key West as a sonar operator, Staley was assigned to Norfolk where he attended destroyer school. In December 1943, he boarded the USS *Stern* DE-187, on which he served for two years and four months traveling to ports all around the world providing escort service against submarine and air attacks. (Courtesy of the Zellwood Historical Society.)

William Davis "W.D." Lovelady was an aircraft mechanic in the Army Air Corps. After basic training at Camp Blanding in Clay County, Florida, and aviation maintenance school, Lovelady served in England at RAF High Wycombe with the US Army Air Forces Eighth Air Force, repairing and maintaining P-51 Mustang fighter planes. (Courtesy of the Zellwood Historical Society.)

Robert and Gladys Potter are pictured in 1941 in Brady, Texas. In 1940, Potter trained cadets to fly, and later transferred to the Military Air Transport Command, where he delivered new B-24, B-25, C-46, and C-47 planes around the world. He was then assigned to the China-Burma-India theater. Potter air transported supplies from India to China across the Himalayan Mountains. The pilots flying these dangerous missions were called "Hump Pilots." (Courtesy of the Zellwood Historical Society.)

Local servicemen and their mothers are featured in this c. 1945 photograph taken in Zellwood. From left to right are Marion Sheddan and Louise Allen Sheddan; George Vincent and Annie Vincent; J.H. Brown and Lilly Ethel Brown; Bob Morton, Lou Morton, and Paul Morton; and Edwin Fly, Leila Fly, and Wesley Fly. (Courtesy of the Zellwood Historical Society.)

W.D. Lovelady and two young women stand beside the Zellwood Honor Roll sign that features the names of "our boys and girls in the service." The sign was located on Jones Avenue. Service personnel met the bus to leave for duty on US Highway 441. An Army camp was located in a field on Lake Maggiore not far from this sign. Several blocks away, soldiers attended plays and concerts at Zellwood Elementary School. (Courtesy of the Zellwood Historical Society.)

Sam and Isabel Boone Barber were married in 1942. Maj. Sam Barber served as a flight instructor at the command and general staff school in Fort Leavenworth, Kansas. He trained to fly, as the wing commander, for the second wave of Doolittle's Raid on Tokyo, but the mission was scrubbed. Barber also served on the advisory committee to choose the site for the new Air Force Academy, ultimately selecting Colorado Springs. (Courtesy of Sam Barber.)

Edward Gurney was born on January 12, 1914, in Portland, Maine. He enlisted as a private in the Army in 1941 and saw action in the European theater. Gurney was a tank commander who had been severely wounded by German machine gun fire in the waning days of World War II. He spent two years recuperating at a veterans' hospital. He served in the US Congress from Winter Park. (Courtesy of the State Archives of Florida.)

Pictured at Rollins College in 1947 are, from left to right, Virginia Roush d'Albert-Lake, Dr. Hamilton Holt, and Louise Homer. In 1943, Florida native d'Albert-Lake assisted her French husband, Philippe, with the French resistance, transporting Allied aviators out of France. She was arrested by a German patrol as part of their *nacht und nebel* (night and fog) directive while leading an airman to safety. She was held at Ravensbrück concentration camp and freed at the end of the war. (Courtesy of Rollins College.)

Seen here in 1947, Col. Charles Trexler has just received an honorary degree of doctor of humanities. Trexler served overseas in World War I. In 1940, he left St. James Lutheran in New York to enter active military duty in World War II. He served as chaplain of the 101st Cavalry, as well as at the Army Medical Center, Walter Reed Hospital, Lawson General Hospital, and as post chaplain at Fort Bragg. (Courtesy of the US Army.)

Ens. Dominick Joseph Richard Cerra from New York, pictured here on May 7, 1943, was a Rollins College student from 1939 to 1942. He enlisted on January 8, 1943, as a Navy pilot, training in Grumman F4F Wildcats and F6F Hellcat fighter planes. Cerra was one of 65 men who died in performance of their duty at Naval Air Station Melbourne between October 1942 and February 1946. He died on February 9, 1944. (Courtesy of the US Navy.)

In June 1939, Pres. Franklin D. Roosevelt signed the Civilian Pilot Training Act of 1939 into law. The law strengthened the national defense prior to entering World War II. The act allowed the Federal Aviation Administration's (FAA) predecessor, the Civil Aeronautics Authority (CAA), to expand an experimental program to train civilian pilots through educational institutions. Rollins College flight school was held at Orlando Municipal Airport. (Courtesy of Rollins College.)

In 1940, with Europe at war, the US Army Air Corps took over the Orlando Municipal Airport for defense purposes, activating it as the Orlando Army Air Base. The first Army Air Corps planes arrived in September 1940, and the base became the interceptor command school. In 1947, a section of the base was used as the Orlando Air Force Base, and in 1968, the base was transferred to the US Navy. (Courtesy of the State Archives of Florida.)

The STAR (Specialized Training and Reassignment) adult education program was established by the US Army during World War II to meet wartime demands for junior officers and soldiers with technical skills. The program, which trained students in engineering, foreign languages, and medicine, was conducted at many universities, including Rollins College. Pictured is the Rollins STAR class in January 1944. (Courtesy of Rollins College.)

At Lake Eola Park in Orlando stands a memorial dedicated to the gallant men and women who participated in the Battle of the Bulge. It features a six-foot-tall bronze statue of a soldier on a granite base. The memorial was erected by the Veterans of the Battle of the Bulge Central Florida Chapter No. 18 and was dedicated on the 55th anniversary of the battle's launch, December 16, 1999. (Author's collection.)

The Apopka Veterans Memorial is located in Kit Nelson Park, which is situated off Park Avenue between First Street and Orange Street. This monument, created by Preston Willingham, was donated by the Veterans Memorial Association of Apopka and dedicated on Veterans Day in 1988. It honors all five branches of the military, with their emblems cast in bronze on each side of the flagpole base. (Author's collection.)

Six

VOLUSIA COUNTY
THE FULLNESS OF BEING HUMAN

The DeLand Naval Air Station (DNAS) Museum is located at the DeLand Airport, the former site of the DeLand Naval Air Station that operated there from 1942 to 1946. The building that houses the museum dates back to 1926 and is listed in the National Register of Historic Places. In 1994, local veterans and volunteers began restoration of the house to use as a museum to honor veterans. The museum was dedicated on November 11, 1995. (Author's collection.)

Capt. Charles "Chuck" Downey (left, pictured with Larry George) entered the Navy in October 1942. He was commissioned on July 16, 1943, becoming the youngest Naval aviator officer of World War II; he was just a few months younger than future US president George H.W. Bush. Downey was a dive-bomber pilot aboard the aircraft carrier USS *Ticonderoga* and then the USS *Hancock*. He flew the Curtiss SB2C Helldiver. Downey received the Distinguished Flying Cross for action in sinking the Japanese cruiser *Kiso* in the Philippines in 1944. In that strike, he lost squadron mate Johnny Manchester. Downey also was decorated with the Air Medal for hangar destruction in Tokyo. Pictured below on January 29, 2014 in Florida are, from left to right, President Bush, Downey, Downey's daughter Elaine, and First Lady Barbara Bush. (Both, courtesy of Charles Downey.)

Pictured at the Ronald Herman Restoration Building at the DNAS Museum in November 2015 are, from left to right, Gene Storz, Chuck Downey, and Elmer Pegram with Rosie. Storz entered the Navy in 1942. He was a structural mechanic on PBYs and B-24s manufactured by Consolidated Aircraft. Pegram entered the Army in 1944. He was a tech sergeant serving at the 5th Replacement Depot in the Philippines; he helped move troops back to the United States. (Author's collection.)

Ken Torbett (right) was a chief petty officer stationed at the Naval Air Station DeLand from 1942 to 1944. He served as a flight line chief and supervisor of flight operations. Torbett kept airplanes ready for pilot training sessions and oversaw the operation of keeping airplanes loaded with ammunition and flight ready. Torbett is a founding member of the Deland Naval Air Station Museum. (Courtesy of the DNAS Museum.)

Clarence L. Hershberger enlisted in the Navy in 1943 and served until February 1946. He was a survivor of the USS *Indianapolis*. While traveling unescorted to the Philippines just after midnight on July 30, 1945, the CA 35 cruiser was hit by two torpedoes from a Japanese submarine. Around 12:30 a.m., the ship capsized and sank 12 minutes after being hit. About 880 men were left floating in the water. When a bomber pilot accidentally discovered them on August 2 while on patrol, 317 were left, including Hershberger. He described his days in the water as being filled with "horror and confusion," and he narrowly escaped shark attacks. Hershberger earned five Battle Stars. The USS *Indianapolis* Memorial, pictured below, is located on the promenade along the Indiana Central Canal. (Left, courtesy of Juaneta Herschberger; below, courtesy of Dina Grenier Peterson.)

Kathleen Ann Knopp Hawver served as a nurse during World War II. She was stationed at the Naval Hospital Camp Lejeune at the Marine Corps base soon after the hospital opened in May 1943. Hawver was one of 90 nurses on staff when the hospital was commissioned. After the war, she continued to work as a nurse for over 30 years. (Courtesy of Zelia Sweett.)

Lady Marine

This c. 1944 photograph shows Lawrence "Larry" Jack Sweett with dog Trooper. Sweett served in the Navy on board the USS *Earl V. Johnson*. He was an electrician's mate (EM3) on the DE-702 escort ship, which was assigned patrol duties in the Philippines and supported the invasion of Okinawa and air strikes on Japan. On August 4, 1945, the *Earl V. Johnson*, despite being damaged, won a three-hour duel with a Japanese submarine. (Courtesy of Zelia Sweett.)

Charles P. Baily served with the 99th Fighter Squadron Tuskegee Airmen. He flew a total of 133 combat missions. Baily named his aircraft after his parents: one bore the name *My Buddy* and the other *Josephine*. In 1945, he received the Distinguished Flying Cross for participating in aerial flight in the Mediterranean theater of operations, during which he demonstrated the highest order of skill, heroism, leadership, and devotion to duty. (Author's collection.)

Richard Fava is pictured with his bride, Helen Hall, in 1945. Fava was a Navy pilot aboard the USS *Bonhomme Richard* and the USS *Lexington*. In one of his last missions, Fava, flying his Grumman TBF-1 Avenger, helped sink the Japanese battleship *Hyuga*, just days before the United States dropped the atomic bomb at Hiroshima. Fava received the Navy Cross for his role in that mission on July 24, 1945. (Courtesy of the DNAS Museum.)

James S. McGee enlisted in the Army in June 1942. In 1944, he became a member of the historic 3rd Infantry Regiment, nicknamed "the Old Guard." Early in 1945, McGee landed at Saint-Lô, France, and was then transported by railroad to the front at Bad Kreuznach, Germany. One week before the war ended, McGee was admitted into the hospital and released after 10 days. He hitch-hiked back to headquarters via the Autobahn. (Courtesy of Jim McGee.)

Don Fuller enlisted in the Navy in 1942. His first combat duty station as a naval aviator was at Kodiak, Alaska. Fuller flew reconnaissance aircraft, gathering intelligence and mapping out safe routes. He flew reconnaissance missions during the Korean and Vietnam Wars as well. In 1956, Fuller acted as an ambassador for the United States to negotiate the return of Japan's offshore islands. He was ordained a Lutheran priest in 1975. (Courtesy of Don Fuller.)

Jack Fortes, second from left, was stationed at the Naval Air Station DeLand from 1945 to 1946. He was assigned to the repetitious duty of packing parachutes. In later years, recollections of liberty weekends were more profound in his memory than his job. He also served on the New Hebrides Islands in the South Pacific. Pictured with Fortes are, from left to right, Jimmie Hines, Hank Cummings, and Kenny Deal. (Courtesy of the DNAS Museum.)

Jack Jarvis, pictured with his wife, Edith Larweth Jarvis, enlisted in the Navy in July 1935 and served for 30 years. He was assigned to the Naval Air Station DeLand when it opened in 1942. During the war, Jarvis participated in the Bougainville Campaign, the Salamaua-Lae Campaign, Battle of the Coral Sea, and Midway. The Jarvises' four sons were all career Navy men as well. (Courtesy of the DNAS Museum.)

Warner Sebra McIntosh, pictured with his grandmother, Rosetta May Bennett McIntosh, enlisted in the Army on October 20, 1942. He trained at Camp Blanding. A native of Daytona Beach, McIntosh was a warrant officer in the US Army Military Police Corps. He was not able to serve in a combat role due to the loss of his eye as a child. He was stationed for most of his enlistment in Gainesville. (Courtesy of Zelia Sweett.)

Fabian Henry Hoffman was an All-American football player at the University of Pittsburgh from 1936 to 1939. He married his college sweetheart, Bernice Kuehner, in 1943. He originally had been rejected by the Army for flat feet, but in 1942, when the heat of war allowed for rejected applicants to serve, he enlisted in the Navy. Hoffman was sent to Naval Air Station DeLand for cadet flight training and was a physical training instructor. (Courtesy of the DNAS Museum.)

Lt. Ruth Lundvall (standing) is pictured here with WAVES at the Naval Air Station DeLand. Lundvall was the administration and public relations officer at the Naval Air Station DeLand. Her duties included assisting civic organizations and war bond committees in fundraising efforts, as well as assisting with applications for WAVES to be assigned to overseas duty. In 1944, nine Naval Air Station DeLand WAVES were approved for duty in Hawaii, Alaska, the Panama Canal Zone, and Bermuda. (Courtesy of the DNAS Museum.)

Sen. Claude Pepper (second from left), along with officials and friends, inspects the Ponce de Leon Inlet in 1945. The men are aboard an aircraft vessel rescue (AVR), commonly called a "crash boat." These boats were small and fast and were used for rescuing pilots from downed planes. The AVR 661 was manufactured in 1943 for the Army Air Corps and used in the Gulf of Mexico. (Courtesy of the State Archives of Florida.)

Seven

MARION AND CITRUS COUNTIES
DUTY, HONOR, COUNTRY

This World War I and World War II Memorial is located in the square at the Old Courthouse Heritage Museum in Inverness. It is dedicated to the residents of Citrus County who "died that we may live" during these global conflicts. This memorial is a twin monument to the Korea and Vietnam Memorial that also stands at 1 Courthouse Square. (Author's collection.)

In 1944, Ralph Esterling (front) received his combat orders that sent him to New Guinea. He flew P-40s and P-38s with the 49th Fighter Group. Esterling served with several highly decorated combat aces, including Richard "Dick" Bong and Tommy McGuire Jr. He witnessed General MacArthur pin the Medal of Honor on Dick Bong. Pictured with Esterling in 1944 are, from left to right, Bob Gustafson, Charles Jones, and George Bower. (Courtesy of the State Archives of Florida.)

Flora "Flo" Reed Walter, pictured at left with Sanda Mott, was a native of Marion County. From 1945 to 1947, she served as a communications specialist (SPQ2) in the Navy. Walter was active in many community and heritage organizations, including the United Daughters of the Confederacy, WAVES National, the American Legion, and the World War II Memorial Society. She is buried in the Florida National Cemetery in Bushnell. (Courtesy of Sanda Crabtree Mott.)

R. GRENIER.

In 1945, while flying his B-51 from Iwo Jima on his 17th mission, Marcus McDilda was shot down off the coast of Japan. He was picked up, blindfolded, and paraded through the streets of Osaka, being beaten and stoned along the way. At the Japanese intelligence headquarters, McDilda was questioned about the A-bomb that was dropped on Hiroshima two days prior to his capture. With the Kempeitai interrogators unsuccessful, an officer was called in. The officer unsheathed his sword and pressed it to McDilda's lip, drawing blood, and threatened to behead him if he did not tell them everything he knew about the atomic bomb. McDilda, remembering his chemistry, spun a lie that he credits with saving his life. The interrogators also wanted to know the next target. McDilda told them that Tokyo and Kyoto were next. McDilda spent 21 days as a prisoner and was liberated from Omori by the 4th Marine Regiment after the Japanese surrender. Many of his captured comrades were not as fortunate, having been executed shortly after the broadcast of the Japanese surrender. (Artwork by and courtesy of Bob Grenier Sr.)

Pictured in Chicago in October 1945, Claude Jesse Mills (fourth from left) is seen after completing cadet pilot training at the Army Air Forces Training Command at Chanute Field, Illinois. Air corpsmen pictured with Mills are, from left to right, "Rigger" Monahan, Joe Nagle, unidentified, William Carmicle, Richard Ogdon, and Benny Knok. Carolyn and Claude Mills are pictured below on their wedding day, September 18, 1954. Mills attained his second class airman's license in 1946, and Carolyn, a Purple Heart Supporter and former secretary of the Yankee Air Force Inc. Florida Division, was a two-time gold medal roller-skating champion in the 1950s. (Both, courtesy of Carolyn and Claude Mills.)

Dear Gen. Tibbets:

    Though we fought in the same war, and indeed in the same service, your contribution far out weighed what we did in the 11th, awaiting our assignment to cover the landings on the main islands of Japan. Your incredible achievement in the Enola Gay not only won World War II but, in due time, the Cold War as well ... without firing a shot. I think it would be fair to say that no single mission in the whole war counted so much.

    I'm glad to have the chance to congratulate you and only wish I could be present at the Yankee Air Force dinner honoring you.

Best wishes,

Charlton Heston

On January 27, 2001, the Yankee Air Force Florida Division hosted a fundraising dinner and dance at the Marriot Hotel in Ocala. The event was called "Salute to Freedom," with a special appearance by Gen. Paul Tibbets. Tibbets was the pilot who, in his B-29 Superfortress the *Enola Gay*, dropped the first atomic bomb on Hiroshima. Carolyn Mills, as secretary of the Yankee Air Force, wrote to actor Charlton Heston requesting a few words from the screen legend (above) that they may present to Tibbets. Heston, best known for portraying Biblical and heroic characters, also served in World War II. He was a radio operator and an aerial gunner with the 77th Bombardment Squadron. In the letter pictured at right, Carolyn Mills thanks Heston for his letter and photograph, as well as for the surprise telephone call she received from him. (Both, courtesy of Carolyn and Claude Mills.)

YANKEE AIR FORCE, INC.

Florida Division

Carolyn Mills-Secretary
8185 N. Fanita Dr.
Citrus Springs, Fl. 34434-5813
352/489-3120
Fax-352/489-3120
c2mills@att.net

Mr. Charlton Heston
2859 Coldwater Canyon
Beverly Hills, Ca. 90210

February 3, 2001

Dear Mr. Heston,

May I first say what a joy it was to speak with you on the phone. As you caught me totally off guard and it was somewhat hard to hear you on the speaker phone, I truly hope I did not sound like a completely overwhelmed fool. (Even if I was.)

General Tibbits was thoroughly delighted with your letter and picture, although he did say he had some help winning the war. You will also see at the end of the video tape I am sending you , the General said, "I always liked Moses!" He, along with the 300 people present was very impressed that you took the time to write a letter and send a photo. I felt that would be a highlight for him as he gives many presentations, (159) last year, and this would be a special moment for him along with the gratitude of all present. He is a very unpretentious gentleman and extremely sharp for his years. I learned his 86th birthday is this month.

I thank you again Mr. Heston for helping me make a special tribute to a gentleman that all of America owes a great deal to.

If I may impose one more request upon you, I would be very grateful if you have another photo you could send to me. You truly have always been one of my favorites. The video is not professional, but my husband is working on perfecting the quality of his films. Once again, Our sincerest thanks,

Carolyn
and Yankee Air Force Members

Richard "Dick" Irving Whittington joined the Marines at the onset of the US entry into the war and served through 1946. He was assigned to the Quartermaster Division stationed at Pavuvu. Whittington participated in the invasion of Okinawa and the Battle of Guadalcanal, acting as a stretcher bearer for the dead and wounded. Whittington was then assigned to the occupation of China in Tientsin for four months, prior to returning to the Unites States. His commanding officer was Gen. Pedro del Valle, who has the distinction of being the first Hispanic Marine general. In 1936, Whittington married Martha Cade Thrasher. The photograph below of the couple was taken around 1948. Whittington served for 13 years as mayor of the Marion County city of McIntosh. (Both, courtesy of the Micanopy Historical Society Archives.)

George Hausold served in the Army Air Forces from 1942 to 1945 with the 465th Bombardment Group. Hausold is pictured above behind the wheel and is seen below at far right in the second row. On June 30, 1944, he was flying his 20th mission when his B-24 was hit by German Focke-Wulf 190 fighters over Hungary. He bailed out, clearing the plane just as it exploded. Ten of the twelve crewmen made it out of the plane. The navigator, who managed to escape the plane, died from his burns 10 days later. Hausold spent the next 10 months as a prisoner of war, which included a stay at Stalag Luft III, best known for two famous prisoner escapes. Pictured with Hausold in the jeep at Pantanella Field in Italy are, from left to right, Jerry Canyock, Louis Kursk, John Fandrey, and Albert "Shack" Myers. (Both, courtesy of Veni and George Hausold.)

Florence Chromulak McCann enlisted as a Navy WAVE on June 19, 1943, and was sent to Hunter College in the Bronx, New York. After a few weeks there, she was transferred to the Navy Secretarial School at Oklahoma A&M College in Stillwater. In November 1943, McCann was assigned as a yeoman third class to the Navy Bureau of Ships in Washington, DC. Her initial quarters were at the Anacostia Navy Base and then permanent quarters at the New Colonial Hotel. On a chance meeting, Florence met her future husband, Bob McCann (pictured below), while walking to her hotel. Bob was an aviation ordnance man stationed aboard the escort carrier USS *Block Island*. He returned from Kwajalein Island in January 1946, and Florence was discharged from the WAVES on February 13, 1946. They were married on February 16, 1946. (Both, courtesy of Florence McCann.)

Eight

ALACHUA COUNTY
JOHN 15:13

The Waldo Veterans Memorial was erected by the Waldo Chamber of Commerce and dedicated on December 7, 1993, to commemorate the 50th anniversary of Pearl Harbor. It is located in historic Waldo City Park. The veterans' memorial also honors police and firefighters. Pictured in the foreground are the Third National (left) and First National flags of the Confederate States of America. (Author's collection.)

Milton Lewis served in the 5th Marine Regiment, 1st Marine Division. Lewis landed on Tulagi on August 7, 1942. On that day, his squad was under heavy fire. He single-handedly charged a Japanese machine gun nest that blocked his unit's advance. Lewis was mortally wounded but was the inspiration for his men, who wiped out the Japanese emplacement. Lewis was the first from Gainesville to be killed in the war. (Courtesy of Fred Donaldson.)

Walter Eugene Olliff, pictured with his sister-in-law Pennie Olliff, was an Army sergeant in the 47th Infantry Regiment, 8th Infantry Division. He died in Belgium on September 22, 1944, just prior to the German offensive campaign at the Battle of the Bulge. Olliff is buried in Henri-Chapelle, Belgium, and was a recipient of a Purple Heart, a Combat Infantry Badge, and an American Campaign Medal. (Courtesy of Pennie and Leon Olliff.)

Bob Gasche enlisted in the Marine Corps in March 1943 at Savannah, Georgia. After boot camp in San Diego, he was assigned to Camp Pendleton, California, for combat training as a rifleman in the 5th Marine Division. On February 19, 1945, his division hit the beach of Iwo Jima. The 5th Division sustained the highest number of casualties of the three Marine divisions engaged. After two weeks of combat, Gasche was wounded, operated on, and then sent back to the United States toward the end of the war. Gasche is the recipient of many awards, including the Purple Heart, Combat Action Ribbon, and the Presidential Unit Citation. Following the war, he received his degree from the University of Florida. In 1951, he served for one year with the 1st Marine Division during the Korean War. (Both, courtesy of Bob Gasche and Fred Donaldson.)

To lift the spirits and release the youthful exuberance of the young servicemen, recreational centers were opened throughout the United States and Florida, including this servicemen's center in Gainesville. Thelma Ann Boltin was the director of the recreation department's program in Gainesville. Today, it is called the Thelma A. Boltin Community Center and is the home of the Gainesville Old-Time Dance Society. The Gainesville Servicemen's Center opened in July 1943 through the joint efforts of the Gainesville city commission and the federal government. Local citizens formed a Girls Service Club and the Masonic lodge provided dormitory space. Dancing to live bands, the Victrola, and the jukebox was the most popular activity. (Both, courtesy of the State Archives of Florida.)

On July 23, 1943, Sen. Claude Pepper dedicated the Gainesville Servicemen's Center. Servicemen from Camp Blanding, the Alachua Army Air Base, the officer candidate school, and the 62nd College Training Detachment attended and participated in events organized by Thelma A. Boltin (1904–1992). Indoor activities included theatrical productions, variety shows, sing-alongs, board games, and cards. Outdoor activities included badminton, shuffleboard, and barbecues. The building included a ballroom, stage, dressing rooms, telephone booths for long-distance calling, a 20-foot-long snack bar (above), and a second-floor reading room, where soldiers could write letters home (below). (Both, courtesy of the State Archives of Florida.)

Across the country, chapters of the American Red Cross were instrumental in the war effort. Pictured in front of the Log Cabin Café in Micanopy are ladies who rolled bandages. They are, from left to right, (first row) Clara Smith, Maude Hillery, Cade Thrasher Whittington, and Maude Davis; (second row) Loraine Chamberlin Howell, Edna McCredie Merry, Ida Perry, Belle Hunter, Rae O'Neal Thrasher, and Fannie Nowlin. (Courtesy of the Micanopy Historical Society Archives.)

Joe Nowlin Chamberlin (third row on the far left) enlisted in the Navy in February 1936. He was a chief water tender in charge of tending the boilers in the ship's engine room. Chamberlin died from injuries sustained from an explosion in the South Pacific on January 20, 1945. His actions in saving the lives of two crewmen earned him the Silver Star. He was the only Micanopy resident killed in action during the war. (Courtesy of the Micanopy Historical Society Archives.)

Nine

FLORIDA'S GALLANT SONS AND DAUGHTERS

In November 2012, the Tavares City Council approved a request by public works director Chris Thompson to erect a large American flag in the roundabout at Sinclair Avenue and Main Street. On February 16, 2013, the "Freedom Flag" was raised with patriotic fanfare. The Freedom Flag Monument was installed on November 21, 2013. The foundation for the monument was built by Tavares mayor Robert Wolfe, Jim Dolan, and David Clutts. (Author's collection.)

This monument, located in the Veterans Memorial Plaza in Merritt Island, honors the thousands of war dogs that have served in military combat. The two most famous World War II dogs were Chips, a collie–German shepherd–Siberian husky mix who was the most decorated dog of the war, and Smoky, a Yorkshire Terrier who saw action in the Pacific theater and participated in a dozen combat missions and survived more than 150 air raids. (Courtesy of Alma Nevarez Grenier.)

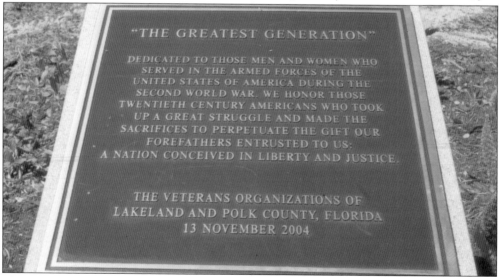

This monument at Veterans Memorial Park in Lakeland pays tribute to "the Greatest Generation." This popular term was conceived by journalist Tom Brokaw to describe the generation who grew up during the Great Depression and then went on to fight or contribute during World War II. The plaque is dedicated to those who made the sacrifices to perpetuate the gift of the United States' forefathers—a nation conceived in liberty and justice. (Courtesy of Carolyn Warner McGraw.)

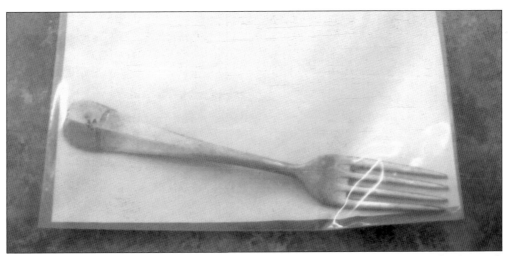

This fork was issued to George Hausold while he was a prisoner of war. Thousands of aircraft were shot down over Europe, which resulted in an abundant supply of aluminum. The Germans recycled the scrap to make pans and cutlery for troops and prisoners. Notice the swastika on the handle. Pictured below are items worn by Hausold. His prisoner-of-war tag had perforations, so that if he died, the tag could be firmly placed in his mouth for easy identification. The American dog tags of World War II had a distinctive notch. The popular explanation for the notch is so the tag could be securely wedged in the teeth of a fallen soldier to insure identification. The notch may have been used to align the tag in an embossing machine. Also pictured are Hausold's bombardier wings and a pendant given to him by his mother, Theresa, in 1943. (Both, author's collection.)

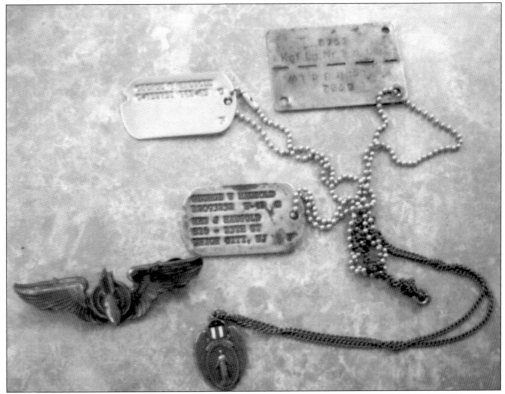

The 124th Infantry Regiment of the Florida Army National Guard is seen marching in London, England, around 1945. The 124th was inducted into service on November 25, 1940, at various Florida stations, including Orlando, Sanford, and Starke. The regiment trained at Camp Blanding and then at Fort Benning, Georgia. Their motto is "Florida and country." In 1945, the 124th Regiment saw heavy fighting on the Island of Mindanao, especially in the Battle of Colgan Woods. (Courtesy of the State Archives of Florida.)

This c. 1942 photograph shows a victory drive for the war effort at Florida State College for Women. Victory gardens, also called war gardens, were gardens planted at private residences and public parks to supplement food rationing. The gardens were planted to take pressure off food production. Gas rationing, as well as rubber, paper, scrap metal, and tin can drives, helped conserve resources and made each home-front American feel like they were contributing. (Courtesy of the State Archives of Florida.)

Victory over Japan Day, also known as V-J Day, was celebrated throughout the peninsula of Florida in August 1945. The photograph at right shows Navy sailors exuberantly celebrating V-J Day in Miami, and the photograph below features women service personnel marching in a victory parade in Tallahassee. On the afternoon of August 15, 1945, the Empire of Japan announced its surrender, which essentially ended the war. On September 2, 1945, the surrender document was signed aboard the USS *Missouri*, officially ending the war. In Japan, the official name of Victory over Japan Day is translated as "the day for mourning of war dead and praying for peace." (Both, courtesy of the State Archives of Florida.)

The January 27, 2001, official show program for the Yankee Air Force Florida Division features Gen. Paul Tibbets and his famous B-29 Superfortress the *Enola Gay*. General Tibbets was the keynote speaker for the Salute to Freedom fundraising dinner and dance. He waived his fee so that all the proceeds could go to constructing a military aviation museum. (Courtesy of Carolyn and Claude Mills.)

The theme of the 38th annual Pine Castle Pioneer Days held on February 26–27, 2011, focused on saluting the men and women of the Pine Castle Air Force Base and Pine Castle's involvement in World War II. The 5th and 99th Bombardment Squadrons operated from the Pine Castle Army Airfield during the war. The squadrons were equipped with B-24 Liberators, B-25 Mitchells, B-26 Marauders, and B-17 Flying Fortresses. (Courtesy of the Pine Castle Historical Society.)

Lt. Allen Putnam (center) is pictured with unidentified pilots at the Sarasota Army Air Field. The airfield was leased to the Army Air Corps by the Sarasota-Manatee Joint Airport Authority in February 1942. The 97th and 92nd Bombardment Groups, as well as the 337th Fighter Group, were assigned to Sarasota. In 1946, the base was transferred to the War Assets Administration (WAA) for disposal and returned to civil use. (Courtesy of the State Archives of Florida.)

This PBY Catalina was one of the various rescue aircraft flown by David Bartelt. Bartelt, the author's uncle, enlisted in the Army Air Corps in Chicago on April 18, 1941. Bartelt served in the Emergency Rescue Service (ERS) of the Army Air Corps and was assigned to the Pacific theater on search-and-rescue missions. One of the pilots in his group discovered the survivors of the USS *Indianapolis*. (Courtesy of Miriam and David Bartelt.)

LN Woods, pictured with his first wife, Genevieve, in 1946, served in the Army Air Corps. Born in Mulberry, Florida, Woods entered the Army on November 7, 1941, one month prior to the Pearl Harbor attack. When Woods enlisted, the Army would not believe that LN was his actual first name. During his career in the service, he was stationed at Eielson Airbase outside Fairbanks, Alaska, various other stateside bases, and Japan. (Courtesy of Dorothy Woods.)

Bruce Harrod Williams (right camel) graduated from the Merchant Marine Academy in 1943 with a degree in steam and diesel engineering. Following graduation, he entered the Merchant Marines as a seaman second class. Williams was stationed aboard the Liberty Ship SS *Jubal A. Early* and the US Army transport *James Parker*. He was awarded the Merchant Marine Combat Bar for service aboard a ship engaged in direct action against the enemy. (Courtesy of Maria Trippe.)

Florida first lady Mary Agnes Groover Holland, along with her daughters, was very active during the Florida war efforts. Holland is pictured above (center) with two telegraph machine operators, and below, she is attending a fundraising event. Mary Agnes Groover Holland served as a plane spotter, grew a Victory Garden at the governor's mansion, knitted squares for soldiers' quilts, regularly attended relief efforts, and supported women in the service. She was born in 1896, grew up in Lakeland, and attended Florida State College for Women. She married future governor Spessard Lindsey Holland in Lakeland on February 8, 1919. The couple had four children. (Both, courtesy of the Polk County History Center.)

Capt. Colin Purdie Kelly Jr. was a B-17 pilot in the Army Air Corps. On December 10, 1941, while stationed in the Philippines, Kelly's crew flew a bombing mission to attack Japanese ships off the coast of Luzon. They spotted a ship they believed to be the battleship *Haruna* and dropped three bombs. The ship was not the *Haruna* but possibly a large Japanese transport or the cruiser *Ashigara*. On their return to Clark Field, a Japanese fighter severely damaged their bomber. Kelly ordered his crew to bail out, but he was unable to exit before it crashed, killing him instantly. Kelly received the Distinguished Service Cross for sacrificing his life so that his crew could live. The Four Freedoms Monument (below) was dedicated in 1944 to his memory. It is located in Four Freedoms Park in downtown Madison. (Both, courtesy of the State Archives of Florida.)

Parker Lee McDonald enlisted in the Army in 1943. McDonald, pictured in Germany in 1945, married Velma Ruth Wilkie of Jacksonville in 1949. The following year, he received his law degree from the University of Florida. In October 1979, McDonald was appointed to the Florida Supreme Court by Gov. Bob Graham. He served until May 31, 1994, which included two years as chief justice from 1986 to 1988. (Courtesy of the State Archives of Florida.)

The Kinsey family are, from left to right, James Leon Kinsey Jr., born February 7, 1944; Laura Louise Loos Kinsey; and S.Sgt. Leon Kinsey. Laura and Leon were married on November 15, 1942, in Lake Charles, Louisiana. He lived in Bell, Florida, until he entered the Army. He served in Germany and was in the medical field. When Kinsey left the military, he lived and worked in Trenton until his death. (Courtesy of the State Archives of Florida.)

Stationed at Pavuvu are, from left to right, Joe Dewhirst, G. Al Scott, Bill Cumbaa, Hank Grasse, Noel Stocker, and ? Robbins. Located northwest of Guadalcanal, Pavuvu is the largest of the Russell Islands. In May 1944, Pavuvu became home to the 1st Marine Division. One Marine remembered, "It was a tropical hole infested with sand crabs and covered with coconut plantations. But at least it was free of Malaria." (Courtesy of Carolyn and Bill Cumbaa.)

Virgil Butler (second row on the left) and fellow officers are photographed in China in April 1944. Kweilin, China, was one of the 14th Air Force's largest bases. Butler recalls in his memoirs, "The 23rd Fighter Group was headquartered at Kweilin, which contained two runways made of mud and rock. P-40s were lined up along the sides. There was an 'alert shack' near the runway for pilots who were on duty." (Courtesy of Miriam Butler.)

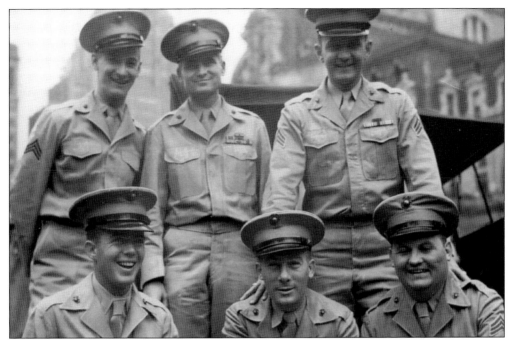

Edward Phifer (at center in the second row) and staff are seen here in Japan around 1945. Phifer kept extracts from the diary of Japanese soldier Hanazono Fujio, dated February 1, 1945–March 1, 1945, at Iwo Jima. Hanazono wrote on February 20, "The attack is so frightful that it seems as if it must change the shape of the island." On February 23 he wrote, "Enemy warships and planes around us here on Iwo Jima on all sides." (Courtesy of Rebecca Phifer Williams.)

William John Hemmen (second from left in the first row) was a sergeant in the Army, serving in the Philippines. He met Margaret Kathleen Doyle in Detroit before the war, but they did not marry until September 1946. Hemmen wanted to wait until he was back home, as not to make Margaret a widow should something happen to him. This photograph, featuring Peso the dog, was taken in Seoul, South Korea, around 1946. (Courtesy of John Hemmen and Kathleen H. Carlson.)

Ray Burtoft (left) and crewmen of the 8th Tank Battalion are pictured with their Sherman tank. The M-4 Sherman tank was present in every theater of operation. It utilized a crew of five, including a commander, driver, codriver, loader, and gunner. Lt. Col. Creighton Abrams was considered the best tank commander in the Army by General Patton. Abrams and his crew, in his M-4 Sherman tank *Thunderbolt*, destroyed an estimated 50 German armored fighting vehicles. (Courtesy of Ray Burtoft.)

The USS *William T. Powell* was a DE-3 Navy destroyer escort. It was named in honor of William T. Powell, a gunner's mate, who was killed in action aboard the USS *San Francisco* near Guadalcanal on November 12, 1942. This c. 1944 photograph of the *William T. Powell's* crew includes future Oveido mayor Leon Olliff, somewhere amongst the many faces of the officers and sailors. (Courtesy of Pennie and Leon Olliff.)

This c. 1943 photograph features a training pilot with a Stearman PT-17 at Dorr Field in Arcadia, Florida. The PT-17's role during the war effort was immeasurable, and by 1940, production soared. More than half of the pilots who fought received their initial flight training in this aircraft. The PT-17 was a biplane with two open cockpits with the student sitting in front and the instructor in back. (Courtesy of the State Archives of Florida.)

Military policeman Warner McIntosh is pictured astride his Harley Davidson motorcycle. The WL model motorcycle, especially designed for the US Army, was produced from 1942 to 1945. 70,000 were manufactured during this time. The Army used the motorcycles for transporting messages between command posts and escorting motor convoys. Their slim build allowed them to travel areas larger vehicles were unable to maneuver. (Courtesy of Zelia Sweet.)

Charles Lindbergh (left) was a military advisor during World War II. Although a civilian, the famed aviator flew about 50 combat missions in the South Pacific. Maj. Thomas B. McGuire Jr. (center) was killed in action on January 7, 1945, and was posthumously awarded the Medal of Honor. McGuire was one of the United States' most decorated fighter pilots and was the second-highest scoring American flying ace of the war. (Courtesy of the US Air Force.)

Greg "Pappy" Boyington is pictured signing copies of his book *Baa Baa Black Sheep* at the Homestead Airport in 1979. Boyington was a Marine Corps fighter pilot and a recipient of the Medal of Honor. In September 1943, he became the commanding officer of Marine Fighter Squadron No. 214, best known as the "Black Sheep Squadron." On September 16, 1943, Boyington shot down five Japanese Zeros in a single engagement. (Courtesy of the State Archives of Florida.)

Famous American generals pictured here are, from left to right, James Van Fleet, George Smith Patton Jr., and Dwight David Eisenhower. The hard-driving, tough-talking Patton said, "It is foolish and wrong to mourn the men who died. Rather we should thank God that such men lived." Future president Dwight Eisenhower said unfalteringly, "We are going to have peace even if we have to fight for it." (Courtesy of the Polk County History Center.)

In 1899, Albert Hazen Blanding was commissioned captain in the Florida National Guard. He commanded the 2nd Florida Infantry in the Mexican Border Campaign from 1916 to 1917, as well as several brigades in World War I. Blanding served on the Florida Selective Service Board during World War II and was appointed by Pres. Franklin D. Roosevelt as chief of the National Guard. Camp Blanding, located near Starke, was named in his honor. (Courtesy of the State Archives of Florida.)

This sketch by Bob Neary, titled the "Blizzard March," depicts the first evacuation march of Allied prisoners of war from Sagan to Spremberg, Germany. POW Neary wrote, "That first night will be remembered for the relentless drive into the teeth of the snowladen wind . . . [and] the men sprawled in the snow, exhausted and utterly oblivious of near-zero temperature and the drift." Neary died in Lee County in 1997. (Author's collection.)

This sketch drawn by Colin Allen was given to Jim Buckner on March 25, 1945. One of Buckner's assignments during World War II was as a Marine Corps barber. Buckner attended barber school following his discharge on November 10, 1945. A photograph of the young barber manning an antiaircraft gun appeared in the December 29, 1941, issue of *Life* magazine. (Courtesy of the St. Cloud Heritage Museum.)

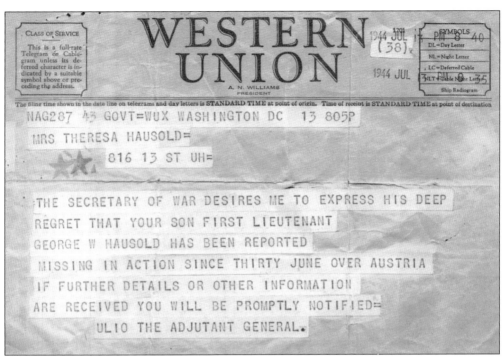

CLASS OF SERVICE

This is a full-rate Telegram or Cablegram unless its deferred character is indicated by a suitable symbol above or preceding the address.

WESTERN UNION

1944 JUL 13 PM 8 40

(38)

A. N. WILLIAMS
PRESIDENT

1944 JUL 13 PM 8 55

SYMBOLS

DL = Day Letter

NL = Night Letter

LC = Deferred Cable

NLT = Cable Night Letter

Ship Radiogram

The filing time shown in the date line on telegrams and day letters is STANDARD TIME at point of origin. Time of receipt is STANDARD TIME at point of destination

NAG287 43 GOVT=WUX WASHINGTON DC 13 805P

MRS THERESA HAUSOLD=

816 13 ST UH=

THE SECRETARY OF WAR DESIRES ME TO EXPRESS HIS DEEP
REGRET THAT YOUR SON FIRST LIEUTENANT
GEORGE W HAUSOLD HAS BEEN REPORTED
MISSING IN ACTION SINCE THIRTY JUNE OVER AUSTRIA
IF FURTHER DETAILS OR OTHER INFORMATION
ARE RECEIVED YOU WILL BE PROMPTLY NOTIFIED=
ULIO THE ADJUTANT GENERAL.

In July 1944, this Western Union telegram was delivered to Theresa Hausold, mother of Army Air Corps pilot George Hausold. Families of servicemen feared the arrival of the "messenger boy on his bicycle" delivering a telegram. It usually meant that their son or husband was killed in action or, as in the case of Theresa; that they were missing in action. (Courtesy of Veni and George Hausold.)

Mail call! "Mail was indispensable. It motivated us. We couldn't have won the war without it," one infantryman remembered. Mail was the lifeline that held the hopes and the will of the servicemen and their worried families together. Between June 15, 1942, and the end of the war, more than 556 million pieces of victory mail were delivered to servicemen overseas, who then sent some 510 million pieces in return. (Courtesy of Margaret "Marli" Wilkins Lopez.)

1st Lt. Alice "Martha" Dorn, pictured here around 1940, was a native of Miami. She attended Ponce de Leon High School and the University of Miami. She was the first female officer candidate in the Marine Corps Women's Reserve from the 3rd Naval District. Dorn became a company commander and then a battalion commander and worked in the Women's Recruiting Depot. (Courtesy of the State Archives of Florida.)

Sarah Golson Kaplan was a 2nd lieutenant in the Army Medical Corps. She served as a nurse and was selected for duty overseas. Kaplan served under General Patton and tended to those wounded in the Battle of the Bulge. She married Army surgeon Samuel Kaplan. In 1949, the couple moved to Venice, Florida. Samuel Kaplan was the first doctor to practice in Venice and was instrumental in starting the first hospital there. (Courtesy of the State Archives of Florida.)

This 1942 photograph shows women lined up at the Civic Exhibition Center in St. Petersburg to register for volunteer service to aid in the war effort. World War II spurred extensive home-front civil defense efforts. Citizens who had not joined the nation's armed forces were eager to support the troops. They joined civil defense organizations in their local communities, volunteering to help construct bomb shelters and to distribute survival information. (Courtesy of the State Archives of Florida.)

Pictured at the China Clipper in Washington, DC, in 1945 are, from left to right, sisters Pat and Marge Naughton, Florence Chromulak, and unidentified. These women served as WAVES and were assigned as office personnel at the Navy Bureau of Ships (BuShips) in Washington, DC. The Navy Bureau of Ships was established in the Department of the Navy in June 1940 and was responsible for the design, structural strength, and seaworthiness of all Navy ships. (Courtesy of Florence McCann.)

Florida representative Darren Soto of Orlando is pictured addressing the surviving members of Puerto Rico's 65th Infantry Regiment in 2009. Sitting with the veterans of this famous regiment is Florida governor Charlie Crist (white suit). A documentary dedicated to the heroic story of the 65th was viewed at this gathering. The 65th Infantry Regiment, known as the Borinqueneers, served during World War II and the Korean War. Pictured below at a reunion in Puerto Rico in 2015 are Osceola County resident Angel Luis Mendoza (far left) and other veterans of the 65th. Mendoza is the only veteran in this photograph who served in both World War II and Korea. (Above, courtesy of the Foley Collection, State Archives of Florida; below, courtesy of Angel Luis Mendoza.)

Proud sons, prouder dads! Seymour and Morris Edelstein are pictured below in Miami Beach, March 1945. Seymour, who enlisted that same year, is wearing his World War II Navy uniform, and his dad, Morris, is wearing his World War I Army uniform. Morris and his wife, Mary, had an older son as well named Harold. Morris was a Russian immigrant who was naturalized in 1939. Pictured at right in 1943 is Marine corporal Arthur Dreves with his dad, George, at the home of his youth in Little Neck, Long Island, New York. George is wearing Arthur's overcoat and cap. (Right, courtesy of Arthur Dreves; below, courtesy of the State Archives of Florida.)

Minnie Engler (cutting cake) organized volunteers to entertain servicemen through the Dade County Defense Council. This c. 1943 photograph, taken at the Thirty-Sixth Street Airbase in Miami, also features Minnie's daughters Molly and Ida (first and third from left). With her sister and mother, Ida founded the Englerettes, a hospitality group of young Miami women. She became the first female police officer in Miami Juvenile Bureau in 1946. (Courtesy of the State Archives of Florida.)

Ray Burtoft (second from right) and comrades from his battalion enjoy some downtime away from their workhorse Sherman tanks. Organizations such as the Young Men's Christian Association (YMCA) and United Service Organizations (USO) sent entertainers and recreation workers to warzones. They opened canteens where soldiers could enjoy hot coffee and donuts, play games, engage in conversation, and when possible, find a momentary reprieve from the war. (Courtesy of Ray Burtoft.)

Lt. Col. Dave Ecoff (with guitar) and fellow unidentified airman were known as the "New Guinea Heart-Throbs." Ecoff was a member of a band called the Valley Vagabonds when they were stationed at the airfield base in Nadzab, New Guinea, in 1944. The group performed live on Armed Forces Radio. Ecoff's military adventures are told in the book *Descending To Go Above & Beyond* by Donna DiMascio. (Courtesy of Chuck Varney.)

The Daytona USO Center also assisted black convalescent servicemen. This World War II–era photograph features the center's director Rebecca Beard Jones (second row on the left) and Gwen Leapheart (second row on the right). Although the military was not legally desegregated until 1948 by President Truman, the USO served black servicemen from the outset. By 1943, more than 180 of 1,326 USO operations were designated specifically for black service personnel. (Courtesy of the State Archives of Florida.)

The Florida National Guard enjoy Christmas dinner in Winter Haven around 1943. As with most wars, World War II did not take a holiday. The Armed Services Command provided holiday meals wherever possible. Those serving on ships and bases, either at home or abroad, as well as those on the front lines, had meals of turkey and ham with all the fixings. Many bases arranged Santa visits, concerts, and parties. (Courtesy of the State Archives of Florida.)

Servicemen march in the Independence Day parade in Orlando in 1943. Independence Day commemorates the July 4, 1776, date on which the Second Continental Congress approved the Declaration of Independence, announcing the 13 colonies' freedom from the rule of the British Empire. During World War II, the United States and England were allies for the same cause of independence, as the future of freedom was uncertain around the world. (Courtesy of the State Archives of Florida.)

The Victorettes Club is pictured participating in an Easter program at the servicemen's club on Calhoun Street in Tallahassee in April 1945. The Victorettes Club was an organization for young women who volunteered to put on shows, host special events, and participate in sporting activities for the entertainment of troops on leave during the war. The Victorettes had clubs throughout the United States. (Courtesy of the Granger Collection, State Archives of Florida.)

A large number of service personnel of the Jewish faith served during the war. In this 1943 photograph, soldiers and their families attend a Seder in Tampa. A Seder is a ceremonial meal held on the first night of Passover commemorating the Exodus of the Jews from Egypt. At a Seder, the story of the Israelites' liberation from bondage is retold, which took on an ironically significant meaning during World War II. (Courtesy of the State Archives of Florida.)

Veterans Memorial Center
Merritt Island, Florida

The Veterans Memorial Center is located in Merritt Island. The center is home to a military museum with an extensive inventory of artifacts from veterans and collectors that pertain to all the wars involving US service members. The center also houses a military library and an auditorium with a picturesque view of Sykes Creek. The jewel of the center is the Veterans Memorial Plaza, which features monuments and military equipment. (Courtesy of the Veterans Memorial Center.)

This World War II monument is located in the Veterans Memorial Plaza at the Veterans Memorial Center on Merritt Island. The monument, with the powerful backdrop of a Navy aircraft and Army tank, is inscribed with the major battles and campaigns of the European and Pacific theaters of operations. Commemorative bricks honoring service personnel pave this inspiring and patriotic plaza. (Courtesy of Alma Nevarez Grenier.)

On December 12, 2015, the town of Micanopy dedicated this veterans memorial. World War II veteran Bob Gasche served as the master of ceremonies, and Vietnam veteran Jim Lynch gave the dedication address. The heading inscribed on this impressive monument reads, "Time will not dim the glory of their deeds." The memorial is also a reminder that "the actions of American veterans continue to preserve equality and freedom throughout the world." (Courtesy of John E. Thrasher III.)

This veterans memorial was erected in 1987 at Veterans Park in Lakeland. The poignant etching on the monument depicts a grieving soldier kneeling by a fallen comrade. The moving inscription on the memorial reads, "For your tomorrow they gave their today." The monument was erected by the veterans of Polk County, as well as the county veterans' organizations and their ladies' auxiliaries. (Courtesy of Carolyn Warner McGraw.)

Albert James "Pedro" Chestnut Jr. of Lakeland joined the US Army and served in the 346th Infantry, 87th Division, as a staff sergeant. On January 9, 1945, he was killed in action at the Battle of the Bulge. Chestnut was laid to rest at the American Cemetery at Luxembourg. The three men in this c. 1945 photograph were Chestnut's friends; they sent this photograph and others to his parents to show them where Pedro was buried. (Courtesy of Patrick Lombardi.)

The author is pictured in 2015 at the Winter Park Cemetery gravesite of Samuel Isaac and Isabel Boone Barber. Barber resided in Osceola County when he enlisted in the Army Air Corps on March 27, 1941, at McDill Field. The Barbers were descendants of Florida pioneering families dating back to the 1840s. Samuel was the great-grandson of cattle baron Mose Barber, and Isabel was the great-granddaughter of Capt. Melton Haynes. (Author's collection.)

The Department of Veterans Affairs (VA) furnishes upon request, at no charge, a headstone or marker for the unmarked grave of any deceased eligible veteran in any cemetery around the world, regardless of their date of death. The VA maintains many national cemeteries specifically devoted to veterans, including the Florida National Cemetery in Sumter County, where World War II veteran Paul Mott (right) is interred. In 1941, the use of granite materials for stones was approved, but by 1947, they were discontinued for a while due to the high cost. The photograph below shows the VA headstone of World War II veteran Thelma E. Mills at the Tavares Cemetery in Lake County. (Both, author's collection.)

Will Rogers said, with candid humor, "We can't all be heroes because somebody has to sit on the curb and clap as they go by." And Harry Truman eloquently said, "Our debt to the heroic men and valiant women in the service of our country can never be repaid. They have earned our undying gratitude. America will never forget their sacrifices." Indeed, we must stand up and cheer, as our soldiers honored us with their service, so we must take the time to remember, honor, and thank them. In 2005, Earl Morse of Ohio cofounded a national organization called Honor Flight. His intention was to fly veterans to Washington, DC, who were incapable of getting there to visit the National World War II Memorial. Pictured are Polk County veterans preparing to depart on the November 2013 Honor Flight. (Both, courtesy of Carolyn Warner McGraw.)

The first Honor Flight took place in May 2005 and is now a national network with over 130 hubs in 50 states. The 24-hour whirlwind journey begins around 1:30 a.m. for the honorees. In Central Florida, they depart aboard buses to Orlando International Airport. Honor Flight, along with local community organizations, businesses, dignitaries, friends, and family members provide a ceremonial send-off. Each of the veterans is accompanied by a guardian on this unique trip to Washington, DC. A medical team also travels with them. The emotional tour begins with a stop at the World War II Memorial and includes visits to the Korean War Memorial, USMC Memorial (Iwo Jima), the Air Force Memorial, and then Arlington National Cemetery to witness the changing of the guard. Pictured are scenes from the November 2013 Polk County Honor Flight bon voyage. (Both, courtesy of Carolyn Warner McGraw.)

Together again! New Smyrna Beach resident Jim McGee (second from the left) is seen having a laugh with men he enlisted in the Army with back in June 1942. The men were attending a World War II veterans reunion at the University Club in Pittsburgh, Pennsylvania. The veterans in this 2004 photograph are, from left to right, Herb Joseph, McGee, Stanley Moravitz, Ed Dardanell, and Sy Sikov. (Courtesy of Jim McGee.)

World War II Navy veteran Laurence Sweett is a descendant of a New Smyrna Beach pioneering family. His mother, Zelia Wilson Sweett, was a noted historian who collected artifacts from the St. Johns River. Much of her collection is on display at the New Smyrna Museum of History. To honor his mother, Sweett continued to preserve New Smyrna Beach history. Pictured with Sweett in 1993 is his daughter Zelia. (Courtesy of Zelia Sweett.)

Groveland resident Ray Burtoft receives the Legion of Honor with the rank of chevalier from Consul General of France Philippe Letrilliart during a ceremony in Ormond Beach on June 30, 2015. The Legion of Honor medals are presented to those World War II veterans who liberated France. Frank Scobby initiated the award process for Burtoft and was his guardian on the Honor Flight in 2013. (Courtesy of Ray Burtoft.)

Navy veteran Richmond "Rick" Lisle Brumby is the assistant director and historian for the Museum of Military History in Kissimmee. Brumby, pictured here at the museum in 2015, comes from a long line of military service dating back to the War Between the States. He is a lifelong martial artist and instructor and uses Rucksack marching as a vehicle to promote veterans' causes and to teach young people the value of service. (Courtesy of Alma Nevarez Grenier.)

Margie Stewart was a model, actress, and the only official US Army poster girl during the war. She appeared on 12 posters, 94 million copies of which were distributed. In 1943, Stewart traveled around the country to sell war bonds. She was one of four starlets, which included Betty Grable, on the tour called "Bondbardiers." In 1945, she was one of the first civilians to enter Germany after the war's end. (Courtesy of the US Army.)

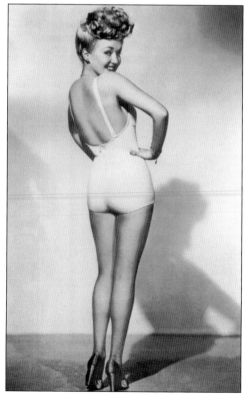

In the six months prior to the attack on Pearl Harbor, three movies starring Betty Grable were released, including the musical *Moon Over Miami*. Grable went on to become the most recognized film actor during World War II. In 1943, Frank Powolny took photographs of Grable in a tight, one-piece bathing suit. When this photograph was released, it became the most requested pinup for soldiers, selling millions of copies and surpassing Rita Hayworth's 1941 photograph. (Author's collection.)

YANK, *the Army Weekly* was the most widely read magazine in the history of the US military. The magazine was produced "by the men . . . for the men in service." Each issue included a pinup girl, usually a screen or stage actress. Many surviving issues of the magazine today are missing the pinup. The cover of this April 1945 issue features the artwork of YANK artist Howard Brodie, who sketched medic Oliver Poythress. (Courtesy of the National Archives.)

Raimund Reischl, from Grainet, Bavaria, served in the German Armed Forces, called the Wehrmacht. He was killed on March 23, 1942, in Russia. Reischl's brothers Leonhard and Franz-Xaver were captured and held in Russian labor camps until the 1950s. Following the war, America saw a surge of German immigrants who wished to escape its aftermath. Many German soldiers who were held in Florida POW camps remained and made Florida their home. (Courtesy of Andrea Seitz Binkley.)

On December 7, 1941, Japan attacked Pearl Harbor hoping to destroy the US Pacific Fleet in one bold strike. Maj. Theodore G. Sharpe of Lake County was at Wheeler Field in Hawaii and remembered, "At 0755 Sunday morning, I was outside the kitchen, waiting in line for breakfast. The line of soldiers was straffed by diving airplanes. I reported to the motor pool and was dispatched to Pearl Harbor, which was a maze of burning ships, running sailors, and straffing and bombing planes. I was assigned to a Liberty Boat and toured the harbor helping pull wounded and dead out of the water." The photograph above depicts the USS *Arizona* and USS *Oklahoma* burning. The photograph below shows a destroyed naval observation scout plane. (Both, courtesy of the US Navy.)

The Korean "grunt" (left) looked much like his World War II counterpart. Not much had changed in the five years since World War II ended. A war-weary country did not expect to be involved in another conflict so soon. Winter gear became critical in the mountain warfare of 1950. Surviviors of the Chosin Reservoir Operation are now known as "the Frozen Chosin." These sculptures were made by Marine Corps combat artist and Korean veteran John Chalk. (Author's collection.)

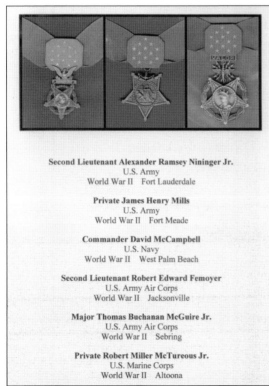

Second Lieutenant Alexander Ramsey Nininger Jr.
U.S. Army
World War II   Fort Lauderdale

Private James Henry Mills
U.S. Army
World War II   Fort Meade

Commander David McCampbell
U.S. Navy
World War II   West Palm Beach

Second Lieutenant Robert Edward Femoyer
U.S. Army Air Corps
World War II   Jacksonville

Major Thomas Buchanan McGuire Jr.
U.S. Army Air Corps
World War II   Sebring

Private Robert Miller McTureous Jr.
U.S. Marine Corps
World War II   Altoona

"For conspicuous gallantry and intrepidity in action at the risk of life above and beyond the call of duty"—Six Medals of Honor for World War II are accredited to Florida. Recipients were 2nd Lt. Alexander Ramsey Nininger Jr., Pvt. James Henry Mills, Cmdr. David McCampbell, 2nd Lt. Robert Edward Femoyer, Maj. Thomas Buchanan McGuire Jr., and Pvt. Robert Miller McTureous Jr. (Author's collection.)

"You're a grand old flag, you're a high-flying flag, and forever in peace may you wave." The Color Guard of the 109th Combat Engineers, 34th Infantry "Red Bull" Division, protect the American flag in northern Italy in 1945. Notice that the flag-bearer is a Japanese American soldier. He served with the 100th Infantry Battalion, which was made up of *nisei*—American-born children of Japanese immigrants. The Stars and Stripes was held in high esteem by the Allied nations around the world during World War II. Flags from dozens of countries, even those that historically were once considered enemies, such as China, the Soviet Union, Great Britain, Iraq, and Cuba, became friends and allies of the United States. Their countrymen, alongside the American servicemen, fought against the evil of the Third Reich and the oppression of the Empire of Japan, even though it meant risking their own lives. They stood with the United States to oppose the Axis powers who tried to take the global freedom away. "OUR Flag—OUR Nation—Under GOD—With Liberty and Justice for ALL." (Courtesy of the Parks family photograph collection.)

On Memorial Day 2015, a dedication of a new headstone for Pvt. Robert M. McTureous was held at Glendale Cemetery in Umatilla. The project to get a new, more substantial headstone for McTureous was led by Boy Scout Micah Martin, who was earning his Eagle Scout rank, and Marine Corps veteran Carl Ludeke of American Legion Post No. 21 in Umatilla. The impressive new five-foot-tall and three-foot-wide monument, adorned with porcelain plaques depicting McTureous, the 6th Marine Division, the Marine Corps seal, and the Medal of Honor, was designed by artist Gene Packwood. Hundreds of people attended the unveiling ceremony, including McTureous's girlfriend at the time he left for service, and Harry McKnight, who served side by side with McTureous at Okinawa. Author Bob Grenier, curator of the Lake County Historical Museum, where McTureous's Medal of Honor is on display, is pictured standing beside the new headstone. Grenier brought the treasured medal to the ceremony and was honored to be the guardian of the Medal of Honor throughout the event. (Author's collection.)

Discover Thousands of Local History Books Featuring Millions of Vintage Images

Arcadia Publishing, the leading local history publisher in the United States, is committed to making history accessible and meaningful through publishing books that celebrate and preserve the heritage of America's people and places.

Find more books like this at
www.arcadiapublishing.com

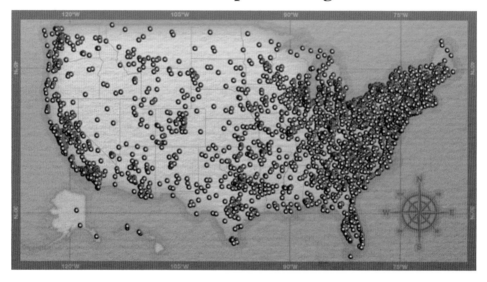

Search for your hometown history, your old stomping grounds, and even your favorite sports team.

Consistent with our mission to preserve history on a local level, this book was printed in South Carolina on American-made paper and manufactured entirely in the United States. Products carrying the accredited Forest Stewardship Council (FSC) label are printed on 100 percent FSC-certified paper.

MADE IN THE USA